Women and War

Women and War

Gender Identity and Activism
in Times of Conflict

Joyce P. Kaufman and Kristen P. Williams

Kumarian Press
An Imprint of Stylus Publishing

Women and War: Gender Identity and Activism in Times of Conflict
Published in 2010 in the United States of America by Kumarian Press,
22883 Quicksilver Drive, Sterling, VA 20166 USA.

The text of this book is set in 11/13 Garamond.

Editing and book design by Joan Weber Laflamme, jml ediset.

∞The paper used in this publication meets the minimum requirements of the American
National Standard for Information Sciences—Permanence of Paper for Printed Library
Materials, ANSI Z39.48–1984

Library of Congress Cataloging-in-Publication Data

Kaufman, Joyce P.
   Women and war : gender identity and activism in times of conflict / Joyce
Kaufman and Kristen Williams.
      p. cm.
   Includes bibliographical references and index.
   ISBN 978-1-56549-309-4 (pbk. : alk. paper) — ISBN 978-1-56549-310-0 (cloth : alk.
paper) 1. Women and war. 2. Women and peace. I. Williams, Kristen
P., 1964– II.
Title.
      JZ6405.W66K38 2010
      305.42—dc22

                                                              2010019627

Contents

Preface

This book is part of an intellectual journey that began in 2000 when we both attended a lecture given by Cynthia Enloe at the University of Southern California in which she admonished the audience to ask ourselves where the women appear in our own research or were they, in fact, invisible. That starting point led to a number of discussions about the absence of women in the work each of us was then doing about the breakup of the former Yugoslavia. Upon realizing that neither of us addressed women within our research, we decided to begin a collaboration in which we examined the impact of the wars in Yugoslavia on women in ethnically mixed marriages, a topic that we both found interesting and that was tied to, although on the fringes of, the work that we were then doing.

That first project grew into a journal article and previous book, and then this research, which grew out of a series of questions that emerged when we explored citizenship and nationalism and the ways in which these become gendered concepts. One of our major areas of interest in that earlier research was to understand the ways in which women become politicized and how that political activism is manifested, especially in societies in conflict. In the course of looking at the four cases that we studied—the United States, former Yugoslavia, Israel/Palestine, and Northern Ireland—we came to some interesting conclusions that led us to ask the question of what happened to the women? In effect, what we saw was that although war and conflict affect women directly, they are generally removed from the decisions that lead to political violence. Yet, they are also significantly affected by conflict and war. In doing the research, we also discovered that even though women were instrumental in working for peace, they often did not enter the formal political structure after the end of the conflict, whether by choice or omission. And this led us to ask why that was the case. Hence, in this book we look at the broad question of what happened to the women: how they were affected during conflict, how they chose to respond politically to their situation, and their status and place when the conflict finally ended.

It is important that we put forward a disclaimer here: as both of us had been trained in traditional international relations, we entered the research about women and gender from that perspective which, we think, gives us a different viewpoint in understanding and writing about women and conflict, including women's contributions to conflict resolution and peacemaking. We think that this book sits firmly at the intersection of traditional and feminist international relations (IR) perspectives. We draw heavily on both the traditional literature and feminist IR theory, which, together provide insights into the gendered notion of the state and decision-making as well as about conflict and conflict resolution.

As we continued the intellectual journey that has led us to this volume, we have sought the advice and counsel of a number of people who have been invaluable sources of support, ideas, and inspiration. Chief among these are J. Ann Tickner, Laura Sjoberg and Cynthia Enloe, all of whom understand our perspectives in approaching this work, and have continually encouraged us to go forward. We also thank a number of people for their valuable comments on earlier versions of this manuscript in the form of conference papers, as well as feedback on individual pieces of this research: Kristyna K. Mullen, Helle L. Rytkonen, and two anonymous reviewers at Kumarian Press.

This research benefited greatly from Joyce Kaufman's trips to Northern Ireland for the purposes of doing interviews as well as archival research. The latter was done at the Linen Hall Library in Belfast, the repository for many of the important political papers documenting the troubles. Yvonne Murphey, the director of development and librarian, Northern Ireland Political Collection, allowed Joyce to have access to the papers of the Northern Ireland Women's Coalition (NIWC), which had not even been archived formally when she was there in June 2008. Alistair Gordon and especially Ross Moore helped sort through the many documents; Ross was especially helpful in trekking up and down stairs with boxes that provided great insight into the NIWC, including the deliberation surrounding its decisions to disband. The countless hours of interviews with women who were directly involved with some aspect of politics in Northern Ireland provided insight that would otherwise have been impossible for someone outside the country. Carmel Roulston, who helped make introductions to many of those women, was once again an important resource. But it was their willingness to give of their time that we especially appreciate. Among those women were Bronagh Hinds, "Catherine," Patricia Lewsley, Jane Morrice, and Margaret Ward. Special thanks to May Da Silva and the group from Women Into Politics who allowed Joyce to participate in the International Women's Peace Conference, Peace by Piece, in Belfast in June 2008. Listening to and being able to exchange ideas with the participants in this conference was a rich and rewarding experience. Also in Belfast, thanks to Audrey, Clare, and Rob, all of whom are or were involved with some aspect of sports and physical activity at the community level, for their insights. They each brought another dimension to an understanding of the Troubles and the divisions in Northern Ireland. Joyce also gives her deepest personal thanks to Joe and Francis and the family for their hospitality during the many visits to Northern Ireland as well as for facilitating a number of contacts. She will never forget the informal concert the family gave at their home one evening, or the promise made during the first visit in 1999 to look into and try to understand more about the Troubles. We hope that this book helps fulfill that promise.

In London, a personal meeting with Cynthia Cockburn was extremely helpful, and we appreciate her time and feedback on our ideas. We also want to thank the staff at The Women's Library of London Metropolitan University for helping Joyce negotiate its archives as well. Although we are both political scientists and not historians, we understand and appreciate the value of primary-source research.

Much of Joyce's travel for purposes of this research would not have been possible without important sources of financial support. In 2007 she was awarded a Small Research Grant from the American Political Science Association to fund some of the travel to Northern Ireland. This was augmented by a Faculty Research Grant awarded by Whittier College; she is grateful to her colleagues for their support of this endeavor. Some of the time spent traveling and writing was made possible because of a sabbatical leave in fall 2007. This, too, would not have been possible without the support of the dean, Susan Gotsch, and especially Ria O'Foghludha, for her willingness to step in and serve as acting director of the Whittier Scholars Program during that semester, thereby relieving Joyce of her administrative responsibilities so that she could travel and write.

Two students, Leslie King (Whittier College, '09) and Deyla Curtis (Whittier College, '12) were instrumental in helping to track down sources and documenting the bibliography. Their help was invaluable, and we appreciate it.

We are also grateful to Lexington Books (an imprint of Rowman and Littlefield Publishers) for granting us permission to reproduce material from *Women, the State, and War* (Lanham, MD: Lexington, 2007).

We owe special thanks to Jim Lance, our editor at Kumarian Press, who has supported this research every step of the way, from our first conversation at an annual International Studies Association meeting in 2007. He has been nothing but helpful and supportive, even when deadlines slipped a bit. Thanks also go to Erica Flock, our production editor at Kumarian Press, who has been incredibly patient with our queries as we moved the book through the production process. As always, even with all the competent and qualified people who read and reviewed all or parts of this volume, any errors or omissions are our responsibility.

No preface or acknowledgments would be complete without thanking our families for their support and encouragement through this next step of our intellectual journey. Joyce Kaufman owes a debt of gratitude to her husband, Robert B. Marks, who accompanied her to Northern Ireland and provided another set of eyes and ears that helped interpret much of what we saw during our many visits. Kristen Williams thanks her husband, James, and children, Anne and Matthew, for their patience and understanding of the time and energy it takes to complete a book.

We dedicate this book to our families and friends, who helped us through this process, but especially, to the women!

Acronyms

ANC	African National Congress
CPA	Comprehensive Peace Agreement
FMLN	Farabundo Marti National Liberation Front (El Salvador)
ICTY	International Criminal Tribunal for the former Yugoslavia
IR	international relations
LTTE	Tamil Tigers (Sri Lanka)
LWI	Liberian Women's Initiative
NIWC	Northern Ireland Women's Coalition
NMA	Naga Mothers' Association
NWUM	Naga Women's Union of Manipur
PLO	Palestinian Liberation Organization
SPLM/A	Sudan People's Liberation Movement/Army
TRC	Truth and Reconciliation Commission
UN Action	United Nations Action Against Sexual Violence in Conflict
UNIFEM	United Nations Development Fund for Women
UNHCR	United Nations High Commission for Refugees

Women and War

Chapter 1

Introduction

Women have long struggled with issues of citizenship, identity, and the challenge of being recognized as equal members of the society. The same society that values and reveres women as symbols used to create national identity ("mother country") as well as for their responsibility for producing the next generation also diminishes or minimizes the role that they play as productive contributors to the society. This duality that surrounds the perception of women is often exaggerated in times of war and conflict where the symbolism—or myths—of womanhood are essential to the very survival of the country. Yet the political reality is such that the decisions regarding war and conflict are generally made by men within the political system from which women are excluded.

The patriarchal nature of most social and political systems often provides barriers to women's involvement in the formal political process, a place in which women could effect significant change. Women frequently are imbued with essentialist characteristics such as peaceful and collaborative, which could be beneficial to the political system under any set of circumstances. At the same time, women are blocked from participating in the political processes that could bring about peace in times of conflict, or that could alter the structure of the system that resulted in the conflict initially.

This leads to a series of questions regarding the political options that are available to women who are affected by conflicts but who are also removed from the political decision-making process that led to the conflict in the first place. Depending on the circumstances, women have four major options for responding to situations of conflict: (1) do nothing, (2) become politically active to help resolve the conflict, (3) actively participate in the conflict as belligerents engaged in violence, or (4) flee the fighting as refugees. Regardless of which option ultimately is selected, women are forced to deal with the situation in some way that requires a conscious choice. And in responding, women have agency.

For this research our primary questions pertain to the ways in which women interact with and then react to the political processes and decisions that affect them

1

at various stages from before the onset of conflict, to the conflict situation, and then the process of conflict resolution and the peacebuilding that follows (in this book we focus on internal/intrastate rather than interstate conflicts). Underlying these series of questions are a number of other equally important questions about women's political activism, specifically what prompts women to take political action at various stages of a conflict, what types of actions they take, and how they can—and do—have an impact when the reality is that, for the most part, they are excluded from political decision-making and mainstream avenues of political power. In this research our focus is primarily on option two of women's possible responses, specifically, women who choose to become politically active in such a way as to help resolve the conflict and then work toward the reconstruction of the post-conflict society.

The central question that has guided the creation of this research is, What happened to the women? We mean that in a number of different ways. What happened to women as a society was building toward war, often something that women can see yet are powerless to stop because of their exclusion from the centers of decision-making? What happens to women during conflict, and how do they react to and cope with situations of conflict? What happened to women during the process of conflict resolution? Do women participate? Do they get seats at the negotiating table? Can and do they make a difference? And, perhaps our most important question, what happened to these same women who engaged in political action specifically to resolve the conflict or for peace during situations of conflict after the violence ends? Do they become part of the system that had previously excluded them? Or do they remain outside the formal political system either by choice or because of structural constraints, or both?

Before we can begin to answer the questions surrounding what happened to the women, it is important to understand the genesis of them. In an earlier book[1] we explored questions about citizenship and nationalism, and the ways in which these become gendered concepts. Major areas of interest were to understand the ways in which women become politicized and how that political activism is manifested, especially in societies in conflict. In the course of looking at the four cases that we studied—the United States, former Yugoslavia, Israel/Palestine, and Northern Ireland—we came to some interesting conclusions that led us to ask, What happened to the women? In effect, what we saw was that although war and conflict affect women directly, they are generally removed from the decisions that lead to political violence. Yet, they are also affected by conflict and war in ways that are different from men who are engaged in the actual fighting. For example, women experience sexual violence such as rape and forced pregnancy, widowhood and becoming heads of household, all of which are largely unique to women.

As a country moves toward war, whether interstate or intrastate, the social and political structure changes, as do the economic priorities, all of which have a direct effect on women. In fact, as a government begins to make the "guns and butter" economic trade-offs that are necessary for a society at war, the social safety net upon which many women depend is removed, leaving them vulnerable while also relatively politically powerless. Cynthia Cockburn notes that the militarization of society "is accompanied by high expenditure on arms." The expenditure on weapons "is often at the expense of spending on public services, including health and education."[2] This is quantifiable and is something that the "average" citizen would notice and experience. Furthermore, these costs are usually borne by women long before war breaks out. According to Jodi York, "Poor women pay it [the costs of conflict] daily when governments divert funds from social services that benefit the poor to defense spending. . . . Since the poor are predominantly women and children, it is from their mouths that social spending is diverted to feed war-making capabilities."[3] Given the economic impact that conflict situations and even the pre-conflict buildup have on women, the question remains what can—or what do—women do to address this?

Similarly, as women work in the community and talk to their neighbors, they are perhaps more sensitive to the changes between or among groups that could escalate into ethnic, religious, or nationalist conflict. Yet, they have few options in addressing these changes. In fact, we could argue, it is women's ability to "dialogue across differences," in the words of Elisabeth Porter,[4] that makes them less willing to accept the notion of "the other"—which has contributed to the proliferation of ethnic and religious conflicts we have seen since the end of the Cold War—and more willing to work for peace.

Once conflict or war erupts within a country, and in this book we focus on internal conflicts rather than interstate conflicts, it is often women who take the lead in pushing for resolution of that conflict or moving the country toward a situation of peace. Research has shown that it is not that women are simply seeking an end to the conflict, but, in fact, that they want to see the post-conflict reconstruction of society address the structural issues that contributed to the outbreak of violence.[5] For women, seeking peace is not just about ending war; it is also about ensuring a system of social justice and equality, eliminating John Galtung's idea of "structural violence,"[6] so that further acts of political violence will be less likely in the future.

There has been a significant amount written about the impact of conflict on women, and we recognize the value of the work that has been and continues to be done in this area.[7] In this volume we draw on a rich body of work but focus specifically on the types of political activism that women engage in at various stages in order to make their voices heard specifically to resolve the conflict. It is important that we make the point here that in describing women's political activism or the ways in which they respond politically to situations of conflict we do not mean to suggest that women were or are passive victims of a situation thrust upon them, although in some cases that might be the case. Rather, our starting assumption is that because women generally have limited input into political decision-making, any actions that they take will be *after* and generally in response to the larger political decisions that were made to engage in conflict at all. In fact, it is in the determination to take action, and in deciding upon the types of actions to engage in, that women gain political power and agency.[8] Or, as Haleh Afshar writes, "Conflicts can both empower and disempower women, since women can be at the same time included in practice and yet excluded ideologically, or they may be both victims and agents of change—though they often have no effective choice in these matters."[9] Women may opt to fight or take action, or they may choose to do nothing. Regardless of which they choose, they will not be untouched or unscathed by the conflict around them.

Similarly, although we generalize and refer to "women" throughout this book, we in no way assert that women are a monolithic group and that all women feel and respond the same ways. In fact, one of the criticisms leveled against mainstream or traditional international relations by feminist IR (international relations) theorists is exactly that: the tendency to generalize across "women" (when women are mentioned at all) thereby minimizing the impact of individual women or groups of women, and also distorting the range of positions that various women hold. Not only do we recognize these differences, but we value the range of opinions and points of view that women have. However, for purposes of our analysis, it is important to identify and generalize the most important strands of thought that women follow while also acknowledging that doing so cannot possibly capture the complexity of the reality.

As Inger Skjelsbaek describes feminism in her report on gendered battlefields: "The feminist activist movement fought for liberation for *all* women in the same manner. In order to achieve this it was important to portray women as a coherent group with similar qualities and problems. It was also important to show that women's interests were qualitatively different from those of men."[10] Hence, generalizing across groups of women becomes an important heuristic device that will allow us to draw important conclusions.

One of the critical decisions that women make is in determining the *type* of actions in which to engage: women supporting war, women opposed to war by virtue of their "motherist" position (that is, building on a more traditional, and essentialist, social role), and those opposed to war for overtly feminist reasons (who may also oppose war in their role as mothers). In the cases of women who opposed war and worked for peace, whether they were motivated by their traditional roles as wives or mothers or because as feminists they opposed the militaristic decisions made by male decision-makers, the immediate goal was the same, and that was to bring an end to the conflict. Yet one can also discern differences in long-term goals. Feminist activists seek to change the patriarchal structure of society and bring about a more just and equal society after the conflict ends. We are interested in the ways women self-identified, and therefore we placed their actions into one of these categories. We are also interested in the *manner* in which women worked for peace. For example, did they work together to begin to facilitate support within their own community? Did they seek to influence the political system by trying to get elected and working within the system as the Northern Ireland Women's Coalition did in responding to the conflict between Catholics and Protestants in Northern Ireland? Or did they remain outside the formal political process but seek to effect change by lobbying or bringing various forms of pressure to bear? And what did women want to accomplish beyond just ending the conflict?

Our earlier research led us to conclude that during conflict, although there are cases where women "clearly put their nationalist identity above gender identity, in many cases those women who were most politically active pursued an agenda that furthered gender identity."[11] In fact, there are numerous cases of women and women's groups who integrated positions that pertained to issues of gender as part of their campaign for peace. For example, initially founded in Israel in 1988 to protest Israel's occupation of the West Bank and Gaza, over time Women in Black broadened its agenda "to protest war, rape as a tool of war, ethnic cleansing, and human rights abuses all over the world."[12]

Conversely, Cockburn addresses the cases of women who elevate their national identity when she writes that "women cannot . . . claim clean hands in the matter of war. They often support belligerent movements." And she supports that claim with some very specific cases, such as "the entirely female elite battalion of suicide bombers of the Liberation Tigers of Tamil Eelam" in Sri Lanka who fought for independence for the Tamils. One of these female suicide bombers assassinated the Indian prime minister, Rajiv Gandhi, in 1991.[13] During the Bosnian War in the early 1990s, which pitted Serbs, Croats, and Muslims against one another, all female militias were also created based on women's national identities.[14]

Clearly, these examples illustrate the range of options open to women in deciding how to respond to or take action regarding their society in conflict. York makes another interesting point about the ways in which women can support war and conflict, albeit implicitly if not explicitly, through the roles that they play in many societies. Oftentimes, women might not see these actions as supporting the conflict as much as taking on important social roles. She notes that "women's support is as necessary to war as that of men; women serve as nurses, prostitutes, primary school teachers who glorify war and patriotic mothers who raise their sons to be soldiers."[15] One could even argue that women are necessary contributors to conflict and war while, at the same time, using many of those traditional roles to fight against it.

Our prior research indicates that during conflict, women often coalesce around a more traditional gender identity, allowing them to pursue issues "as wives" or as "mothers," identities seen as less threatening in a patriarchal structure already deeply divided.[16] This does not preclude women political activists from taking positions and roles that are more overtly political. For example, in Northern Ireland, women were placed on government commissions, such as the Parades Commission and the District Policing Partnerships as well as the Human Rights Commission, all overtly political positions that allowed them to address broader political issues head on.[17] But those tend to be representative of a smaller number of cases than the number of women who joined together in opposition to conflict using a more traditional gender identity as the coalescing force as seen in Northern Ireland and in other countries as well.

Situations of conflict can also cause women to move beyond those traditional roles and take on new ones. As Donna Pankhurst notes, in some cases the circumstances of war and conflict resulted in "moments of liberation from the old social order. As the need arose for them [women] to take on men's roles in their absence, so they had to shake off the restrictions of their culture and live in a new way."[18] In fact, what this means is that whether they wanted to or not, women were often thrust from the private realm into the public, and many found it not only liberating but life changing. It is that political and social empowerment that can take place during conflict that emboldens women to take political action not only during the conflict but subsequently. In this way the binary divide between the private and public spheres is not so clear cut. Rather, the public versus private spheres are better understood as a continuum, with women crossing these spheres.[19]

The essentialist "motherist" position or reliance on a more traditional women's role has advantages for women who opt for political action in both the position it takes (bring an end to the conflict that is killing our husbands and children) and the representation or symbolism that goes with it. This is especially important given the symbolic roles that women often play in spurring a country, a society, or a particular group toward conflict, for example, fighting for the "mother country," or the recognition of "gold star mothers" who sacrifice one or more children for their country.[20] Who, within a society, could object to parents uniting against what many perceived as the unjust Israeli invasion of Lebanon in 1982 (Parents Against Silence), or to the creation of a women's peace movement in Northern Ireland founded by two women "as a response to the deaths of three children struck by an IRA car, whose driver had been shot by an army patrol"?[21] Sanam Naraghi Anderlini's work shows that activists such as the Argentine Mothers of the Plaza de Mayo used their motherhood identity as a means to challenge the authoritarian government's policy of dealing with political dissent in which people "disappeared." A society and regime that espouses "motherhood as the ultimate virtue" faces difficulty in responding to such activism in a heavy-handed manner.[22] Thus, drawing on their common and traditional roles as women often allows groups to coalesce and bring attention to the need to end a conflict in a way that is not perceived as threatening—or is perceived as less threatening—to the dominant political culture or group. Moreover, in "embrac[ing] their gender essentialism," women are expressing their agency.[23]

But as York also notes, this approach poses problems in that "it accepts women's subordinate role in our society. Some argue that doing 'women's work,' rather than making life better or increasing the likelihood of peace, merely collaborates with patriarchy by ameliorating its worst aspects, making patriarchal and militaristic oppression more bearable."[24] Even with agency, using gender essentialisms really only "reinforces patriarchal values and hierarchies." Moreover, as feminists have noted, when women's movements utilize their traditional domestic roles as their identity, these movements, according to Elissa Helms, "are too easily co-opted by patriarchal, male-dominated nationalist movements."[25]

This approach also raises the danger that once the conflict ends, as many scholars have shown, women will be expected to shrink from the spotlight and to return to their traditional (and subordinate) roles once again.[26] However, this traditional route might be the best—or only—option open to engage women in trying to influence the political process, especially women who had not been involved prior to the outbreak of conflict. The challenge is whether long-term structural changes in the society that will elevate women's status and equality can be achieved. Evidence from scholars suggests that such achievement is elusive.

In trying to engage with the political system or with the larger society as a whole prior to or during a situation of conflict, women have another barrier that they need to overcome: "The propaganda machines used by states are too powerful and more prepared than women, who are often stepping into the fray for the first time. National security, typically defined within a military discourse, is not a domain in which women civil society activists feel comfortable."[27] This, too, often propels women to act within the confines of the areas that they know best and in which they are most comfortable, that is, as wives and mothers or within the boundaries of their community, where they can work with a small group of people and can build situations of trust.

Consequently, engaging women in a political response in periods of conflict forces women to address an area that is traditionally defined not only as masculine, but one that is virtually the exclusive domain of men. This further excludes women from decision-making. For that reason, examples abound of women who work within their own communities, often across existing social/ethnic/religious divisions, in order to try to effect change. While this might not change the outcome of the decision to engage in war, conflict, or societal violence, according to Patrick Regan and Aida Paskeviciute, such activities provide additional avenues within which women can have an influence on the political process. They note that "women's potential involvement in the political process" can provide a constraint on the timing of the start of war; in other words, when men make the decision to initiate war. They found that even at the community level, where women's involvement is most likely, women "can have an important influence on government's decisions to get involved in military disputes regardless of regime type."[28]

A country or a society that is in conflict often asks or requires women to take a stand. It is virtually impossible to remain neutral in the face of civil violence that completely disrupts the order of society and where that violence has a direct impact on the women and their families. But, as we saw in our earlier work, even when women do take a stand, they are also often described as "invisible," a word that was used in reference to some women's groups in Northern Ireland[29] and is a theme also seen in a book on women's roles in the Solidarity movement in Poland, for example.[30] Thus, one of the challenges facing women who undertake political action is whether or how to make themselves visible and their presence known at all stages in the continuum from peace to pre-conflict, to war, negotiations, and then, hopefully, back to peace.

In this book, to frame our analysis we draw on traditional IR theories as well as work within the field of feminist international relations. Traditional IR theory does a relatively good job of dealing with issues pertaining to state-building and national security. However, as Tickner notes, "Characteristics associated with femininity are considered a liability when dealing with the realities of international politics." She continues, "When realists write about national security, they often do so in abstract and depersonalized terms, yet they are constructing a discourse shaped out of these gendered identities."[31] When women are injected into the discussion of international relations and issues of conflict, negotiations, and peace, it is often in gendered terms, for example, linking women and pacifism or presenting women as victims.

Utilizing a gendered analysis, feminist IR scholarship provides a challenge to traditional IR to examine the ways that "gender differences permeate all facets of public and private life."[32] As Wenona Giles and Jennifer Hyndman state, "Feminists have long argued that private/public distinctions serve to depoliticize the private domestic spaces of 'home' compared to more public domains."[33] Such scholars have shown that despite the fact that women are often marginalized politically (because women are primarily located in the private sphere), the symbolism of women becomes essential to the survival of the state and nation. Women need to be defended and protected, and it is men who are the protectors, thereby prompting men to support the state's call to war. The private sphere becomes all the more important for control by the public sphere, thus perpetuating the pattern. Even when women enter the public sphere, patriarchy continues.[34]

Consequently, in examining women's behavior and political activism (thereby crossing the private-public divide, or politicizing the private sphere), feminist scholars demonstrate that women engage in antiwar activism for myriad reasons. What is important to keep in mind, as feminist scholars such as Cockburn will attest, is that "feminism sees gender power relations as systemic, not contingent or incidental."[35]

Thus, in examining women's antiwar activism, feminist scholars recognize the gender power dynamics at play. Importantly, feminist scholars use a gender analysis to account for women's activism that opposes war and patriarchy, but also women's activism that supports and reproduces patriarchy, as well as war and militarism.[36]

When women in Northern Ireland, or Israel, or South Africa work for peace in their respective states on the basis of the traditional claims of motherhood (that is, as a mother, I want to assure a better and more peaceful world for my children), they do not necessarily self-identify their actions as feminist per se. Many would argue that they are simply taking a political stand as wives and mothers who want to make the world (or their community, on a more micro level) a safer place for those they love. For these women, feminist political activism is not necessarily their stated rationale for their actions nor is it the way in which they define their actions.[37]

In this research, as we look for answers to what we think are important questions, we are trying to understand the options available to women and why they chose the actions that they did. Importantly, we examine the issue of women's agency. Additionally, we illustrate that the conventional dichotomies of the private versus public spheres are often misleading. Instead, we argue, while patriarchal societies may deem the private sphere the domain of women, what happens in the public sphere affects women as well. Women engaging in political activism further cross that divide when they overtly participate in the public sphere regardless of whether in community-based work, informal political activism, or formal politics.

This research draws on the work of numerous authors who have explored aspects of war and conflict, negotiations, peacemaking and peacebuilding. Where we think this book makes an important contribution is in the ways in which we use women as the central variable. Hence, as we reviewed the literature on peace negotiations, for example, we noticed that it tended to focus on the negotiations per se, without any mention of *who* was sitting at the table or why. In other cases the literature we draw on specifically looked at women's roles in negotiations, but often without placing the negotiations into a broader theoretical framework.

Our goal is to do both things: as we examine the stages of conflict (pre-conflict, conflict, and post-conflict) drawing on the relevant literature, we will also consciously inject the roles of and impact on women. We draw on a range of specific examples from different countries and parts of the world in order to support our conclusions, and from both feminist and traditional IR for our theoretical focus. The result will be a far more comprehensive understanding of women's political activism at all stages.

In order to draw our conclusions, in addition to referring to the relevant literature and applications, we have also been able to interview women who have been involved politically in different countries and at different stages of conflict (the results of some of the specific interviews are highlighted in boxes in Chapters 4 and 5). While these interviews are not meant to be exhaustive, they provide important insights into various political systems, the perceptions of the women, the roles that they could—or could not—play, and the choices that they made once the conflict was resolved.

In Chapter 2 we provide the theoretical framework for this research within the context of both traditional and feminist international relations. The chapter examines the origins of the nation-state, traditional and feminist IR accounts of war, security, and women's political activism. We explore the connections between women's identities and their activism.

Chapter 3 examines the impact of conflict and violence against women in two ways. First, sexual violence, particularly rape, seems part and parcel of most, if not all, conflict. Women are specifically targeted for sexual violence by virtue of the fact that they are women. Whether a systematic policy by leaders or individual incidences of sexual violence, women are targeted during conflict. Second, conflict also affects women when they become refugees. When women flee the violence, they face many challenges, including finding housing, healthcare, employment, and so forth. Further, women refugees are often victims of sexual violence when they leave the refugee camp to find fuel and water.

Chapter 4 focuses on women's political activism during conflict. While the chapter does address women engaging in political activism as belligerents, the focus is on women peace activists. We look at the ways that women form networks at the grassroots level, which in many cases crosses ethnic/national divides. We further examine types of conflicts, both those societies in which conflict is overt and in societies in which there are social and political divisions (and conflict), but violent civil war is not present.

Chapter 5 explores women's political activism in the post-conflict period when women attempt to be active participants in the negotiating process to get to a peace settlement as well as maintaining a presence in the formal political arena. The chapter demonstrates that women also choose to remain in the informal political arena, as well, affecting change from the outside. The obstacles women face in getting a seat at the negotiating table are also presented.

The concluding chapter provides a recap of the main themes of the book, noting the similarities and differences in women's responses in the different stages of conflict, and answering the question, What happened to the women? The chapter briefly discusses areas for future research, particularly the other side of the coin: women who choose violence rather than peace in response to conflict.

Notes

[1] Joyce P. Kaufman and Kristen P. Williams, *Women, the State and War: A Comparative Perspective on Citizenship and Nationalism* (Lanham, MD: Lexington Books, 2007).

² Cynthia Cockburn, "The Gendered Dynamics of Armed Conflict," in *Victims, Perpetrators or Actors? Gender, Armed Conflict, and Political Violence*, ed. Caroline O. N. Moser and Fiona C. Clark (London: Zed Books, 2001), 18.

³ Jodi York, "The Truth about Women and Peace," in *The Women and War Reader*, ed. Lois Ann Lorentzen and Jennifer Turpin (New York: New York University Press, 1998), 23.

⁴ Elisabeth Porter, "The Challenge of Dialogue across Difference," in *Gender, Democracy and Inclusion in Northern Ireland*, ed. Carmel Roulston and Celia Davis, 141–63 (New York: Palgrave, 2001).

⁵ See for example, Tsjeard Bouta, Georg Frerks, and Ian Bannon, *Gender, Conflict, and Development* (Washington DC: The World Bank, 2004); Sanam Naraghi Anderlini, *Women Building Peace: What They Do, Why It Matters* (Boulder, CO: Lynne Rienner, 2007); Swanee Hunt and Cristina Posa, "Women Waging Peace," *Foreign Policy* 124 (May–June 2001): 38–47; Donna Pankhurst, "Women, Gender, and Peacebuilding," Working Paper 5, Center for Conflict Resolution (Bradford UK: University of Bradford, August 2000); and Azza Karam, "Women in War and Peacebuilding," *International Feminist Journal of Politics* 3, no. 1 (April 2001): 2–25.

⁶ Johan Galtung, "Violence, Peace, and Peace Research," *Journal of Peace Research* 6, no. 3 (1969): 171.

⁷ Works on the impact of war and conflict on women over the last few decades are numerous, and address intrastate and interstate wars, both in general and in specific case studies. Examples include Cynthia Cockburn, *The Space between Us: Negotiating Gender and National Identities in Conflict* (London: Zed Books, 1998); Joshua S. Goldstein, *War and Gender: How Gender Shapes the War System and Vice Versa* (Cambridge: Cambridge University Press, 2001); Krishna Kumar, ed., *Women and Civil War: Impact, Organizations, and Action* (Boulder, CO: Lynne Rienner, 2001); Lois Ann Lorentzen and Jennifer Turpin, eds. *The Women and War Reader* (New York: New York University Press, 1998); Julie A. Mertus, *War's Offensive on Women: The Humanitarian Challenge in Bosnia, Kosovo, and Afghanistan* (Bloomfield, CT: Kumarian Press, 2000); Caroline O. N. Moser and Fiona C. Clark, eds., *Victims, Perpetrators or Actors? Gender, Armed Conflict and Political Violence* (London: Zed Books, 2001); Vesna Nikolic-Ristanovic, ed., *Women, Violence and War: Wartime Victimization of Refugees in the Balkans* (Budapest: Central European University Press, 2000); Rosemary Ridd and Helen Callaway, eds. *Caught Up in Conflict: Women's Responses to Political Strife* (London: Macmillan, 1986).

⁸ See Karam for a discussion on the debate regarding women's victimhood versus agency (Karam, "Women in War and Peace-building"), 7.

⁹ Haleh Afshar, "Part One: Introduction, War and Peace: What Do Women Contribute," in *Development, Women, and War: Feminist Perspectives*, ed. Haleh Afshar and Deborah Eade (Oxford, England: OXFAM GB, 2004), 2.

¹⁰ Inger Skjelsbaek, "Gendered Battlefields: A Gender Analysis of Peace and Conflict," PRIO Report (Oslo: International Peace Research Institute, October 1997), 11.

¹¹ Kaufman and Williams, *Women, the State, and War*, 195.

¹² See http://womeninblack.net/mission.html.

¹³ Cynthia Cockburn, "Gender, Armed Conflict, and Political Violence," originally prepared as a background paper for the World Bank (June 1999), 10. A revised version of this

paper was later published as "The Gendered Dynamics of Armed Conflict," in Moser and Clark, *Victims, Perpetrators, or Actors?*

[14] Obrad Kesic, "Women and Gender Imagery in Bosnia: Amazon, Sluts, Victims, Witches, and Wombs," in *Gender Politics in the Western Balkans: Women and Society in Yugoslavia Successor States*, ed. Sabrina P. Ramet (University Park: Pennsylvania State University Press, 1999), 189.

[15] York, "The Truth about Women and Peace," 22. For an extensive examination of the ways that women are militarized in support of war and conflict, see Cynthia Enloe, *Maneuvers: The International Politics of Militarizing Women's Lives* (Berkeley and Los Angeles: University of California Press, 2000).

[16] Kaufman and Williams, *Women, the State, and War.*

[17] The authors wish to thank Margaret Ward for this astute observation in the case of Northern Ireland.

[18] Pankhurst, "Women, Gender, and Peacebuilding," 5.

[19] Tickner makes clear that feminist scholars view the public/private divide as problematic, that the divide reinforces the view that women belong in the private realm and men in the public, and with that conventional view comes the assumption that therefore the public sphere is more important (and worthy of study) than the private sphere. J. Ann Tickner, "You Just Don't Understand: Troubled Engagements between Feminists and IR Theorists," *International Studies Quarterly* 41 (1997): 622.

[20] See Pnina Werbner and Nira Yuval-Davis, "Women and the New Discourse of Citizenship," in *Women, Citizenship, and Difference*, ed. Nira Yuval-Davis and Pnina Werbner (London: Zed Books, 1999). Also see V. Spike Peterson, "Gendered Nationalism: Reproducing 'Us' versus 'Them,'" in Lorentzen and Turpin, *The Women and War Reader*, 41–49.

[21] Begona Aretxaga, *Shattering Silence: Women, Nationalism, and Political Subjectivity in Northern Ireland* (Princeton, NJ: Princeton University Press, 1997), 181n1.

[22] Anderlini, *Women Building Peace*, 38–39.

[23] Elissa Helms, "Gender Essentialisms and Women's Activism in Post-War Bosnia-Herzegovina," in *Feminists under Fire: Exchanges across War Zones*, ed. Wenona Giles et al. (Toronto: Between the Lines, 2003), 181, 192.

[24] York, "The Truth about Women and Peace," 20.

[25] Helms, "Gender Essentialisms and Women's Activism in Post-War Bosnia-Herzegovina," 181.

[26] Karam, for example, notes that "once the struggle is over, women are expected to perform their national and peace-building duties by being good wives and mothers." Among the cases she cites to support this point are Algeria after its civil war, Zimbabwe, Palestine, "and to some extent, Nicaragua" (Karam, "Women in War and Peacebuilding," 10).

[27] Anderlini, *Women Building Peace,* 35.

[28] Patrick M. Regan and Aida Paskeviciute, "Women's Access to Politics and Peaceful States," *Journal of Peace Research* 40, no. 3 (May 2003): 290.

[29] In her study of Catholic women in Northern Ireland, Begona Aretxaga stresses the invisible role that many women played "behind the scenes" that provided the structure that allowed men to continue the fight (Aretxaga, *Shattering Silence*). Where Aretxaga studied primarily Catholic/nationalist women, Rachel Ward, in her study of Protestant/unionist

women, used much the same wording to describe women's political role on that side of the Troubles: "They [women] have varied political roles, although these are often invisible." Rachel Ward, *Women, Unionism, and Loyalism in Northern Ireland: From Tea-Makers to Political Actors* (Dublin: Irish Academic Press, 2006), 11.

[30] Shana Penn, *Solidarity's Secret: The Women Who Defeated Communism in Poland* (Ann Arbor: University of Michigan Press, 2005).

[31] J. Ann Tickner, *Gender in International Relations: Feminist Perspectives on Achieving Global Security* (New York: Columbia University Press, 1992), 41.

[32] Tickner, "You Just Don't Understand, 614.

[33] Wenona Giles and Jennifer Hyndman, "Introduction: Gender and Conflict in a Global Context," in *Sites of Violence: Gender and Conflict Zones*, ed. Wenona Giles and Jennifer Hyndman (Berkeley and Los Angeles: University of California Press, 2004), 3.

[34] See J. Ann Tickner, "Feminism Meets International Relations: Some Methodological Issues," in *Feminist Methodologies for International Relations*, ed. Brooke A. Ackerly, Maria Stern, and Jacqui True (Cambridge: Cambridge University Press, 2006), 38–39.

[35] Cynthia Cockburn, *From Where We Stand: War, Women's Activism, and Feminist Analysis* (London: Zed Books, 2007), 229.

[36] Ibid., 240–41. Contrary to Cockburn's assertion, Carla Koppell, director of the Institute for Inclusive Security at the Washington, D.C. office of Hunt Alternatives Fund, claims that much of the feminist literature makes certain assumptions about women's behavior and women's political activism. By presupposing that all women's political activism is overtly feminist, she argues that the literature misses some of the subtleties that would otherwise help us understand why and how women act in the ways in which they do. Furthermore, it often puts women's attitudes regarding "feminism" or "activism" into a Western understanding of the terms. While many in the West would demean or look down upon women who define their activism based on their roles as mothers, in a non-Western setting many cultures elevate that role, thereby giving women additional status and, with that, credibility to act (the authors thank Koppell for her insights). We have found that many feminist scholars do seek to understand the different motivations women have for engaging in political activism that may be explicitly feminist, or not. See, for example, Amina Jamal's article, which addresses the challenge for feminist scholars to account for women's involvement in Islamic fundamentalist movements in Pakistan. She notes that how these women self-identify "as Muslim blurs the personal and public in ways that conflicts with (Pakistani) feminist accounts of women's autonomy and emancipation and more directly threatens the feminist project in Pakistan. Thus, feminist scholars are forced to offer a different explanation for the religiously defined identity of Jamaat women when it takes the form of public political action than when it is a matter of women's 'personal choice.'" Amina Jamal, "Feminist 'Selves' and Feminism's 'Feminist Representations of Jamaat-e-Islami Women in Pakistan," *Feminist Review* 81 (2005): 67–68.

[37] For a discussion of women in antiwar activist organizations who do not see themselves as explicitly feminist in their activism, see Cockburn, *From Where We Stand*, 207–11.

Chapter 2

Theoretical Framework

Governments, which are almost universally patriarchal, depend heavily on the creation of a national identity that places women at its core (for example, mother country) while at the same time excluding them from participating in critical political decisions. Often the barriers to women's participation in the formal political system are not overt but are imposed by social and political realities. These include the costs and time commitments necessary to run for office, access to networks or mentors who can help provide critical introductions, and meetings scheduled at times when women cannot attend (for example, those with child care and school-aged children), to name but a few of the barriers that inhibit women's involvement with the formal political system.

Despite the fact that they are often marginalized politically, the symbolism of women becomes essential to the very survival of the state.[1] In this argument, which pertains directly to issues of gendered nationalism, women (mother country) need to be defended, and it is men who are responsible for doing so. This puts women into secondary positions in which they are subservient to and dependent upon men while they are also excluded from the heart of political decision-making and from positions of power and authority in the military.[2]

Feminist scholars such as Nira Yuval-Davis, Floya Anthias, Pnina Werbner, and V. Spike Peterson have demonstrated the various ways that gendered nationalism manifests itself. For example, "women as biological reproducers of group members" can be shown through policies enacted that restrict access to contraception and abortion as well as providing material rewards to women from a particular nationalist/ethnic group for having more children.[3] As women become more involved with various political struggles and conflicts, their perceived private role in the family merges further with the public sphere of the nation. As Cockburn notes, "The more regressive the rendering of national community, the more does nation involve reproductive and familial imagery (birth, blood, sons) and the more profoundly is gender differentiated and essentialized, man as warrior, woman as nurturer."[4] The need to preserve and promote the nation and its cultural identity

15

places pressures, therefore, on women to behave in a certain way.[5] Thus, nationalist leaders, namely men, are compelled to oppose those who would challenge the perception of the private sphere of group identity and reproduction of the members of that group that emanates from women's role in the family.[6]

In the context of conflict, gendered nationalism is also evident when we observe "women as participants in political identity struggles." Women are not just symbols of group identity, but they also support, and oftentimes actively participate in, nationalist causes, including nationalist conflicts. Whether in the form of leading troops into battle or engaged in a supportive role to feed and clothe combatants, women are involved in political struggles and conflict, thus complementing women's perceived role in the private sphere of the family with the public sphere of the nation.[7]

As noted by Tsjeard Bouta, Georg Frerks, and Ian Bannon, these are "patriarchal practices and values that are not easily changed." They use the example of South Africa, where women "have been identified as 'mothers of the nation.'" However, in their analysis "women's practical involvements as well as the ideological discourse employed in defining the sphere of their actions centered on motherhood, responsibility for children, and protection of the family. . . . The discourse was framed within patriarchal boundaries."[8] Consequently, in many cases, the ways in which women have historically fought for social, civil, and political rights both within and outside the formal political structures have been by drawing on a more "traditional" framework in their roles as wives and mothers. The patriarchal nature of most political systems and processes are biased against the formal involvement of women. Especially in more traditional societies, when women's involvement was encouraged (or accepted) at all, it was within the bounds of the more traditional (maternalist/essentialist) framework. This approach to gender roles also reinforces the notion that it is the men who go out and deal with the world (the public sphere), including engaging in war and conflict, while women's domain is the private sphere, primarily the home and family. Oftentimes, however, the public converges on the private, such as when homes are bombed or used to store weapons, leaving women little choice but to engage more broadly.

What we are addressing here is the convergence of the traditionally public and private spheres as women who are affected by armed conflict determine how best to address the situation based on decisions that generally are made by men and that threaten their security and the security of those who are closest to them. Implicit in this from a traditional IR perspective is the crossing of "levels of analysis" in that decisions made by the decision-makers affect not only the nation and the society, but clearly individual women who pay the price when the country is in a state of conflict.[9]

J. Ann Tickner explains the relationship in the following way: "Whereas conventional security studies has tended to look at causes and consequences of wars from a top-down, or structural, perspective, feminists have generally taken a bottom-up approach, analyzing the impact of war at the microlevel."[10] What this reminds us of is the importance of looking at the whole picture, at who made or makes the decisions that ultimately result in armed conflict or violence, and who is affected by the decisions that are made.

The chapter, therefore, begins with a discussion of the gendered origins of the state, including a discussion of traditional IR theory as it relates to war. In this section we present the feminist IR critique of traditional IR theory, particularly the ways in which the traditional approach to IR is highly gendered. From this, we move to a discussion of women and security, particularly how security is defined in the traditional literature and how others have sought to expand the definition of security, one that encompasses security at the micro level rather than only at the level of the state. This discussion of security leads directly to an examination of women's identities and how those identities influence women's decisions to engage in political activism. We conclude the chapter with a brief discussion of women's political activism in times of conflict.

The Gendered Origins of the Nation-State

The notion of conflict is as old as written history. Man competing against man (the stories usually involved men), brother against brother, tribe against tribe seems to be a universal given of the human condition. The creation of the nation-state, however, brought with it certain assumptions about the ways in which states could or would intervene or act toward one another, especially regarding situations of conflict and war. Implicit in this is the understanding of the ways in which individuals within the nation-state would or should behave, with men behaving one way and women another. From its creation the nation-state was a gendered concept.

The concept of the modern nation-state has its origins in 1648 with the Treaty of Westphalia, which ended the Thirty Years' War in Europe. In many ways, then, the concept of the state is inseparable from war and conflict. The Treaty of Westphalia took four years to negotiate and was actually a series of treaties that ended the Holy Roman Empire and established new countries in its place. The result was the creation of the modern European state system, although borders and boundaries changed after that time as new countries were created, often as a result of war.

In dividing the empire and creating new states, the treaty also specified a governmental or political order within each of these states as well as the relationship between and among them. Implicit in this was the admonition that each of the members of the governing nobility of the states will leave the others alone; that is, that each noble is free to govern within his borders and that other states shall recognize that. Thus was born the concept of sovereignty.

As K. J. Holsti notes in his classic text on IR, the principle of sovereignty goes back to the Treaty of Westphalia and "the principle [of sovereignty] underlies the relations between all states today." Holsti elaborates: "The principle of sovereignty is relatively simple: Within a specified territory, no external power . . . has the right to exercise legal jurisdiction or political authority. This establishes the exclusive domestic authority of a government. That authority is based on a monopoly over the *legitimate* use of force" (emphasis added).[11] Holsti then notes in a corollary to his definition that "no state has the right to interfere in the domestic affairs of another state. This prohibitive injunction has been breached frequently, but it is assumed and observed most of the time by most states."[12] The point that Holsti also makes is that, despite periodic violations, this concept has guided international relations, that is, relations between and among states, since 1648. It is this admonition of the sanctity of the sovereign state that has made it so difficult for states to intervene even in cases of flagrant abuses of human rights, ethnic cleansing, and so on, which often accompany civil war.

Charles Tilly also makes it clear that there is a direct relationship between state-building and war. In fact, Tilly notes that "from the sixteenth century onward, settlements of major wars regularly realigned the boundaries and the rulers of European states, right up to World War II; the division of Germany, the incorporation of Estonia, Latvia and Lithuania into the Soviet Union, and the dismantling of more European empires overseas all stemmed more or less directly from the settlements of World War II."[13]

It is that militaristic essence of the state that builds a gendered perspective into the concept of the nation-state, as argued by feminist IR scholars who are particularly interested in the connection between masculinity and war, and their impact on women.[14] States are not gender-neutral but, in fact, are gendered entities in that, in Tickner's words, they "promote and support policy practices primarily in the interests of men."[15] Moreover, as the modern (primarily European) state developed in the eighteenth and nineteenth centuries, participation within the polity was limited—only men could participate fully. Tickner contends: "We must conclude, therefore, that the historical construction of the state, upon which the unitary-actor model in international theory is based, represents a gendered, masculine model. In the West, the image of a foreign-policymaker has been strongly associated with elite, white males and representations of hegemonic masculinity."[16] Or, as Gillian Youngs looks at state formation from an explicitly feminist perspective, "The history of state formation and identity is therefore one of gendered (and other forms of) oppression." She continues: "In its range of critical work on the state, feminist International Relations has, directly and indirectly, accused mainstream International Relations of depoliticizing exploitation by ignoring the relational gender dynamics integral to the political power of states as (masculinist) actors."[17]

Furthermore, even the study of the nation-state system and the interactions among states is male dominated. According to V. Spike Peterson and Ann Sisson Runyan, "The preponderance of male scholars and practitioners partly explains the silence on gender: Men checked with each other about what men were doing that was considered relevant to other men and was written by men for primarily male audiences!"[18] They then go on to define what distinguishes international relations from political science in particular, in that the former focuses on relations among states. While not inherently exclusionary, the applications of the concepts became so.

Whereas domestic political observers and policymakers have had to grapple with voting behavior, welfare state issues, domestic public interest groups, and social movements—areas in which gender issues figure prominently—IR practitioners have focused on national security (defined most often in terms of military might), economic power (defined typically by gross national product indicators), and international organizations and regimes (made up of government and financial elites). Not only are women infrequent actors in these matters of state, but IR orthodoxy also sees no place for women in these high-stakes games.[19]

Writing initially in 1948, shortly after World War II and at the start of the Cold War, Hans Morgenthau makes a similar distinction between domestic and international politics, but he frames the differences between the two in terms of the application of power, something that defines the realist school and that generally excludes women. "The essence of international politics is identical with its domestic counterpart. Both domestic and international politics are a struggle for power, modified only by the different conditions under which this struggle takes place in the domestic and international spheres." He then uses a rather gendered example to illustrate the ways in which all human associations, from family through the state, are about the struggle for power: "On the family level, the typical conflict between the mother-in-law and her child's spouse is in its essence a struggle for power, the defense of an established power position against the attempt to establish a new one." However, he does draw the analogy between power at the domestic level and international level when he applies the example, stating that "as such it foreshadows the conflict on the international scene between the policies of the status quo and the policies of imperialism."[20]

If IR seeks to describe and explain the behavior of states (and increasingly non-state actors) within a defined international system, then the critical concepts that govern those interactions are not only power but also security. These concepts have traditionally been steeped in masculine definitions. Morgenthau looks at power as "anything that establishes and maintains the control of man over man. Thus power covers all social relationships which serve that end, from physical violence to the most subtle psychological ties by which one mind controls another."[21] Looking at it from that perspective, power is a relational concept whereby one person/government/country is seeking to influence and control the behavior of another. And while admittedly that approach does help us understand some aspects of the international system or the behavior of nations, as Peterson and Runyan point out, it neglects other components that are also important: "When we use only this narrow definition of power to study world politics, however, we neglect investigating how other dimensions of social reality—moral commitments, religious beliefs, ethnic allegiances, sociopolitical ideologies—shape how power works and who rules the world." And, they also remind us that "this definition of power is masculinist to the extent that it presupposes androcentric notions of strength, competition, aggression, and coercion, and because it focuses on power understood only in terms of public-sphere activities that are dominated by men."[22] In other words, it values or elevates the role of "high politics," or "hard power," at the expense of "low politics," or "soft power."[23] The latter, "low politics" or "soft power," has become especially important in understanding international relations since the end of the Cold War.

Morgenthau outlined the realist paradigm in IR drawing upon the role of "states-*men*" to prove his point. His ideas reinforce the point made by Peterson and Runyan about the gendered nature of the field. "The main signpost that helps political realism to find its way through the landscape of international politics is the concept of interest defined in terms of power." He then continues, "We assume that states-*men* think and act in terms of interest defined as power, and the evidence of history bears that assumption out." Of course, that assumption presumes that it is possible to review all the steps a states*man* takes: "We look over *his* shoulder when he writes *his* dispatches; we listen in on *his* conversation with other states*men*; we read and anticipate *his* very thoughts" (emphasis added).[24] In short, for Morgenthau and the other theorists who helped define the field of IR, the role and/or presence of women was something that was not even considered. Explaining IR and the behavior of states was tied to understanding the way the men who made the decisions think. There was virtually no attention given to the impact of those decisions on the people who were affected by them, nor was there any mention of women either as decision-makers or as members of the society.

Traditional IR Theory and War

Taking this approach another step, traditional realist theory would argue that war is an inevitable result of the competition for scarce resources and power between and among nations. Here Kenneth Waltz draws on the work of Morgenthau and other realist IR thinkers when he says that "power appears as an end-in-itself, whereas a greater emphasis on the first root of political discord would credit power as an instrument necessary for success in competitive struggles." Inherent in this approach are assumptions about the behavior of people as well as the behavior of states within the international system. In both cases the assumption is that each entity will be driven by a desire to maximize power that, in turn, will lead inevitably to conflict, either because "struggles for preference arise in competitive situations and force is introduced in the absence of an authority that can limit the means used by the competitors," and/or "that struggles for power arise because men are born seekers of power." In either case, national interest will be defined in terms of power, either as an instrument or an end.[25]

In trying to explain macro-level issues such as war and peace, Waltz later draws on approaches in behavioral science to help explain these broad concepts. In so doing Waltz offers a number of contending approaches to understand the outbreak of war. In one of these possible explanations he posits the positions of "others" who "argue that wars occur because men expect war; to abolish war, the expectations of men must be changed."[26] This is an interesting assertion; it presumes that war is inevitable because men (and we assume that Waltz literally meant men) are programmed to compete in this violent way.

Waltz's ideas are paralleled by rhetorical questions posed by psychologist J. Cohen, upon whose work Waltz draws. In this case Cohen asks: "Is it not remotely possible that the causes of war intrinsic in a system of sovereign States are the result of the male as against the female 'element' in these societies? Is it not conceivable that wars occur because of the overwhelming influence of *men* in government, administration, and international affairs? Might not a full emancipation of women promote a more peaceful order?" (emphasis added).[27] Waltz then condenses the essence of Cohen's argument by noting that Cohen "believes that the cause of peace might be promoted if women were substituted for men in the governing of nations."[28]

Tickner, in contrast, explicitly introduces a feminist or gendered approach to understanding macro issues of war, peace, and security. She writes: "In looking for explanations for the causes of war, realists as well as scholars in other approaches to international relations, have distinguished among three levels of analysis: the individual, the state, and the international system. While realists claim that their theories are 'objective' and of universal validity, the assumptions they use when analyzing states and explaining their behavior in the international system are heavily dependent on characteristics that we, in the West, have come to associate with *masculinity*" (emphasis added). Tickner continues, "The way in which realists describe the individual, the state, and the international system are profoundly gendered; each is constructed in terms of . . . idealized or hegemonic masculinity. . . . In the name of universality, realists have constructed a worldview based on the experiences of certain men; it is therefore a worldview that offers us only a partial view of reality."[29] Tickner and other feminist IR theorists remind us of the fact that when we study or define war, there is an inherent bias that needs to be addressed if we are to be able to paint a more realistic understanding both of what war is and of the impact that it has on women.

Joshua Goldstein, in his seminal work on war and gender, begins with his definition of war. He goes beyond the "common definition used in political science" of wars with at least one thousand battle deaths,[30] and defines war broadly "as *lethal intergroup violence*" (emphasis in original). More relevant to our work, he notes that "warfare worldwide in recent years has seldom taken the form of pitched battles between state armies." Rather, he continues, the kinds of wars that are more prevalent today are those that "occur between groups (communities, ethnic groups, societies, states)."[31] It is this latter point that is especially important.

Especially since the end of the Cold War, states or groups within states were no longer constrained by the fears that conflict could grow into major war between the East and the West. They were, therefore, more likely to go to war. In addition, the democracy and liberation movements that swept parts of the world following the end of the Cold War also contributed to a growth of nationalist fervor that seemed to induce more ethnic and/or religious groups to clamor for their own state; nations wanted their own statehood. These various factors contributed to the onset of intrastate as opposed to interstate armed conflict and war.

Not all of these cases resulted in armed conflict. For example, the "velvet divorce" that resulted in the peaceful division of Czechoslovakia into the two countries of Slovakia and the Czech Republic is one example. But that is the exception, and is due, in part, to the de facto divisions that already existed or, put another way, to the artificial creation of a single country by imposing a single statehood on areas that were actually already divided.

That case stands in marked contrast to its neighbor Yugoslavia, another country created initially after World War I as a single state with six republics and numerous ethnic groups that lived within those borders. Following Josep Tito's death in the 1980s, and prompted by the growth of nationalist leaders and without a strong central government to hold the republics together, the country exploded into ethnic and civil war in the late 1980s and early 1990s as each of the ethnic groups vied for territory ("Serbia for the Serbs"). That violence was spurred further by the economic downturn that hit parts of former Yugoslavia after the Cold War, when the country was no longer a critical player in the East-West balance of power equation. It did not take long for the concept of being a Yugoslav to morph into the designator of Croat, Serb, or Bosniak (Bosnian Muslim). Along with that came "ethnic cleansing," or the desire to make each area "pure" by removing violently any group that did not belong to the dominant one.

Another type of conflict that proliferated following World War II and that continues in various guises to the present are what used to be called wars of national liberation, or wars for independence. While many of these took place in the 1950s and 1960s under the umbrella of the Cold War, there are many others that continue today or that have emerged since the end of the Cold War. Often the colonial or imperialist power imposed on its colonies the political and social structure that paralleled its own. Hence, the creation of a "have" and a "have not" division that was perpetuated during the fight for independence and subsequent to independence. And, given the patriarchal structure of most of the European colonial powers, women were in general among the "have nots" both during the colonial period and after.

These examples—colonial wars of independence, ethnic, civil, and religious wars—do not discount the societies that were already roiled by violence of some type for reasons separate from the geopolitical changes at the end of the Cold War. And there are numerous examples of these cases as well. Northern Ireland is an example of a society divided by religion. Yet, delving beyond that simple explanation for the Troubles are other causes, both political and economic, that pitted the Protestant majority against the Catholic minority since 1921 and the treaty that granted Ireland "home rule." Similarly, the violence between Arabs/Palestinians and Jews in Israel can be traced to 1948 and the creation of that state, which came at the expense of the Palestinians, who were also promised statehood and who still fight for that goal.

Taken together, these cases all are representative of Goldstein's definition of "lethal intergroup violence" and provide the guidelines for determining which examples we include in our analysis. But another critical factor that characterizes all of these cases is the impact that the violence had on women, who were virtually absent from the decisions to go to war or to engage in conflict.

What has also changed since the Cold War ended has been the distribution of power, not only across but also within nation-states. Increasingly national/ethnic/religious groups within a single state have asserted themselves in an attempt either to gain control of the existing political structure or to break away and create a new national state that is more homogeneous in character. It is this latter desire that has contributed to the growth of intrastate civil conflict that has been especially harsh for women. The underlying concept is the same: the struggle to gain power. But the means by which this has been accomplished has often been especially violent and brutal in its impact on civilians. What makes the escalation of such conflicts especially troubling for the members of the international system is that since they are internal civil conflicts, if other states adhere to the traditional tenets of sovereignty they cannot—or will not—intervene, as evident by the case of the genocide in Rwanda in the mid 1990s, which many states condemned but took no actions to stop.

Placing state actions or inaction into the concept of sovereignty underscores another point that Peterson and Runyan make; that is, it eliminates, ignores, or allows states to abrogate what they call "other dimensions of social reality," such as moral judgments, social justice issues, protection of basic human rights, and so forth.[32] In fact, it elevates sovereignty to a higher value than these others, thereby permitting states *not* to take action even in cases of dire human rights abuses, such as the ethnic cleansing and human rights abuses that took place in Bosnia, Rwanda, and Sudan. It is often in consideration of those dimensions that women seek to inject their ideas either during the conflict, to draw attention to the situation that caused such things in the first place, or in seeking to resolve the conflict and create a post-conflict society that addresses the structural causes that led to the outbreak of violence initially.

Women and Security

If the struggle for power between, among, and within states has traditionally been defined in masculine terms, so has the understanding of security. Again, according to Morgenthau, states seek security defined in terms of power,[33] that is, if a country maximizes its power vis-à-vis other countries, then the perception is such that the country will be more secure. Countries, or more accurately the decision-makers within a country, will act in order to protect that country's core or critical interests. According to Barry Hughes, core interests "flow from the desire [of the state] to preserve its essence: territorial boundaries, population, government, and sover-eignty."[34] What the primary definitions of *security* leave out is how that concept or pursuit of security takes into account the needs of the women within the borders of the country—or does it?

From a very broad IR perspective the concept of security is tied to the need to protect the nation-state and the people who live within its borders. However, any discussion of the concept of security must take into account the fact that the very notion of security has changed to encompass not only broad concepts of national security defined in traditional military terms, but on a macro level, economic issues tied to globalization and trade, and issues pertaining to the environment, health, and the spread of infectious disease, and human rights, that is, issues that can be broadly termed "human security."[35] It is the responsibility of the political decision-makers to oversee all aspects of security that affect the nation-state in general and the people who live within it.

Similarly, at a time when the nature of security is changing on a macro level, we also need to ask how the concept has changed on a more micro level. A report published by the International Peace Research Institute in Oslo, Norway, on gendered perspectives of conflict and peace asks, "Is there a female concept of security?"[36] In the exploration of that question the report concludes that "the attempt to formu-late a feminist security concept is valuable. . . . It highlights the connection between what we normally consider masculine norms and values, and the conventional na-ture of security. The effect is that it reveals the conventional concept of security as gendered and not neutral,"[37] in part because the concept itself is steeped in mascu-line norms. The report also states that "most political decisions concerning war and peace are made by men and that this maintains a male value-system." The report asserts that while there is no guarantee that women's representation in the political sphere will affect the actual decisions made, "an increase in female representation creates a potential for *different* concepts of security" (emphasis in original).[38]

Youngs addresses the issue of security and violence slightly differently when she draws on the feminist perspective specifically. While she acknowledges the centrality of violence and the state to the concept of security in traditional IR, she also makes it clear that "feminists have examined extensively the extent to which mainstream concepts of security in the field have been traditionally constrained by masculinist blinkers, failing to take account of security issues women confront daily that are associated with their unequal or oppressed conditions of existence in relation to men." She notes that war and military occupation, human trafficking, forced migration, and forced prostitution affect women and children in very different and very specific ways. Mainstream understandings of security do not adequately examine those issues.[39]

Peterson and Runyan point out that the "what" of IR is changing, specifically noting that the end of the Cold War and the concomitant changes to the international system "have altered the practical and theoretical terrain of IR. More specifically, peace studies and development studies have challenged conventional definitions of security and economic growth. . . . By focusing on the security needs of people and the planet, these approaches open the field to gender issues."[40] What becomes especially important in any discussion or understanding of security is the distinction that must be made between studying "security" and what it means in terms of IR (feminist or more traditional IR), as opposed to understanding what it means in practice, that is, what people in general, and women in particular, do to ensure their own security and that of their family and community. Or, put another way, it is the difference between theory and practice. Clearly there has been a broadening of the study of security issues to encompass women due, in part, to the work of a number of feminist authors who have helped to redefine the term. Along with that, though, it is important to review and analyze the actions that women took in the name of security.

Thus, in this discussion of conflict, peace, and women, it is important to remember that underlying many of women's actions is the desire to assure security for themselves, their families, their communities, and potentially their country, and that is the goal that they are ultimately working toward. What varies is the ways in which they understand the concept and then choose to pursue and achieve that security, which is often at odds with the primarily masculine concept of the term.

The concept of security has a number of dimensions that have become more apparent after the end of the Cold War and, with that, the changing nature of the international system. One of the other major changes has been in the types of conflicts that have emerged. Here, too, many authors have made the point that as the nature of warfare changed, the dangers to civilians increased. This is especially true of the vulnerability of women and children. For example, Jacobson, Jacobs, and Marchbank write in the "Introduction" to *States of Conflict* that "the nature of warfare has undergone major changes, involving a widescale retreat from even a qualified observance of those historic rules of war which had offered protection to non-combatants. Instead, protagonists deliberately target civilians, including children, using the increasingly available technologies of rocket-propelled grenades, mortars, land mines and small arms."[41] Pankhurst describes this slightly differently when she states, "Where there is no front line, as conflict is fought out in people's homes, with light weapons, and where the reason for fighting is the very existence, or at least presence, of people with a differently defined identity (usually ethnic), women have been placed on one side or another whether they actively choose this or not."[42]

Thus, not only has the notion of security in a traditional sense changed, but conflict and war have intruded upon the personal security of civilians, especially women and children. That personal security is undermined because the rules of engagement have changed, as have the parameters of the battlefield. This has been critical in propelling women into situations of conflict, whether they wanted to be placed there or not.

This has led to other threats to women's physical security, both in terms of personal violation, such as rape—which has increasingly become a tool of war—but also to the threat of violence at home, as domestic violence is clearly linked to social or state-sponsored violence. Here the work of Tickner is instructive. She writes: "Feminist perspectives on security would assume that violence, whether it be in the international, national, or family realm, is interconnected. Family violence must be seen in the context of wider power relations."[43] Hence, women's physical security has become more endangered given the types of conflicts that have predominated within the past few decades.

It is also important to note that economic issues now directly affect women's security. This is not a new concept; women traditionally have been tied to men (husbands, fathers) for economic security and well-being. But the changes in the international system have had an impact on women's economic security, again, in ways that are often beyond their control. Where the concepts of economic security and conflict converge are in the ways in which a militarized society makes economic choices that affect women prior to as well as during and after conflict. As noted above, a society that is gearing up for war makes choices about the expenditure of resources, that is, military needs versus domestic priorities. And in that equation, the domestic side of the equation (butter as opposed to guns) loses.

In his 1969 article, when he introduced the concept of structural violence, Johann Galtung described a situation in which "violence is built into the structure and shows up as unequal power and consequently as unequal life chances." He then continued: "*Resources* are unevenly distributed, as when income distributions are heavily skewed, literacy/education unevenly distributed, medical services existent only in some districts and for some groups only, and so on. Above all, the *power to decide over the distribution of resources* is unevenly distributed" (emphasis in original).[44] In addition to describing a social and political situation predisposed toward violence, clearly, this also describes a situation that is skewed against women, who have the least access to the decisions regarding the distribution of resources.

Drawing on Galtung's concept of structural violence, Cockburn again reminds us of the relationship between political violence and economic distress, which often serves as a precondition for and precursor to actual conflict. Here Cockburn describes violence as existing on a continuum that can be found along multiple dimensions and that is perpetrated by mainstream institutions such as the government and the church as much as by rebel groups, which are often seen as the source of internal political violence. But, perhaps even more important, growing from these works is the conclusion that depressed economic conditions take their toll on women in the home (especially for those who are single heads-of-household), in society, and in the nation, contributing to further inequalities not only between sexes/genders, but also across classes.[45]

An important conclusion is that although the concept of security in traditional IR thinking presupposes that all within the nation-state will benefit equally from the security protections afforded them by the state, the reality is that we must acknowledge that security is gendered and we must look within the state to understand this concept more completely, a point that will affect our analysis of conflict and its effects on women.

Women's Identities and Political Activism

As Chapter 1 indicated, women have different identities, which are salient at different times. We are particularly interested in women's gender identities as well as their national identities. During times of conflict these identities are themselves in conflict. Women may perceive their ethnic/national identity as more important than their gender identity when there is an ethnic/nationalist war. For example, during the Bosnian wars in the early to mid 1990s, women from the three predominant ethnic groups, Serbs, Croats, and Muslims/Bosniaks, attempted to form cross-ethnic alliances to promote peace and protest the wars, thereby finding common ground as women. Yet over time, as the wars continued, these same women found that their ethnic identity was more important than their identity as women, and they became more supportive of their respective ethnic groups. As a result, these cross-ethnic alliances were doomed to fail. What this tells us is that women's identities are not fixed.

At the same time, women's identities are also a focal point for engaging in political activism. One of the interesting points in understanding women's activism as it relates to women's identities is the notion of women's issues. Is there such a thing as women's issues? If so, how are they defined? As Karen Beckwith and Kimberly Cowell-Meyers assert: "The idea of women's substantive [political] representation hinges on the notion of some kind of shared experience among women that fosters a sense of common social or political interests. Because women's experiences are socially constructed and because they vary widely based on the specific processes of construction, women's issues differ from context to context, across and within states and across time."[46] Moreover, class and race enter into the equation in regard to the effects of gender.[47] Beckwith and Cowell-Meyers define policies as women's issues such as those that liberalize divorce and reproductive rights, provide family and medical leave, legislation that criminalizes violence against women, legislation that promotes equal pay, education, property rights, and so forth.[48] In their study of countries with parliamentary political structures, they found that left-wing parties are more likely to advance women's issues (as they define them above) than right-wing political parties.[49] In addition, countries with active feminist movements can affect the policy process through pushing for legislation that promotes women's issues, including "bring[ing] direct pressure upon (or provide immediate support to) elected women, providing them with a political (and often financial) base to strengthen their capacity to advance those issues in parliament."[50] They further show that "in the absence of a feminist movement, supportive public opinion, or a strong left-party to adopt the agenda of women's descriptive representation, women are not likely to be elected in large numbers to the assembly."[51]

It is clear then, that one way that women can engage in political activism is through participation in women's movements. As Beckwith notes, women's movements are important entry points for "democracy at the level of citizen participation," thereby making democracy more inclusive. Women's movements, in essence, "generally extend mass participation and thus contribute to democratic development." Moreover, because all women in a society "share the common experience of political exclusion as a class," they also "share a common focus as they organize." Women seek "to challenge and to transcend their political exclusion as they struggle for specific goals." In doing so, both the state and civil society are confronted by the demands of women's movements to be responsive to those groups who are not normally included in the power structures of the state.[52]

Yet, as Beckwith observes, "definitions of women's movements sometimes serve to conflate feminist movements and women's movements."[53] As she makes clear, women's movements can consist of antifeminist and right-wing women's movements. These types of women's movements address women's issues and "women's gendered experiences" but do not seek to change the patriarchal structure of society. It is feminist movements whose activism seeks to alter existing patriarchal power arrangements based on male domination and female subordination. Feminist women's movements can be understood, therefore, as a subset of women's movements broadly defined.[54] She defines women's movements as *"social movements where women, organized explicitly as such, are the major actors and leaders and make gendered identity claims the basis for their actions"* (emphasis in original).[55] What women's movements have in common, therefore, is that women's issues, decision-making, leadership, and gendered experiences are front and center in their definition.[56]

For feminist movements in many countries, whether in times of conflict or not, the challenge is whether to become active inside the formal structure or remain outside the formal structure. The debate, as Beckwith defines it, is one of autonomy versus coalition in terms of political strategies for changing the patriarchal structure. Thus, should feminist movements form alliances, or coalitions, with political parties (particularly on the left of the political spectrum, to include the creation of a feminist political party or women's party, such as ZEST, the Serbian women's party) and enter into the formal political structure? Or should feminist movements avoid inserting themselves into formal politics and maintain autonomy from the formal political structure?[57]

Beckwith comments that maintaining autonomy enables women's movements to avoid cooptation by the government. In doing so, however, women's movements may end up losing the opportunity to influence the state and its policies.[58] As she further observes:

> Women are located both externally to institutions whose actions they aim to influence (e.g., government agencies) and internally within institutions where institutional membership and participation are the goals (e.g., labor unions, universities). As a result, political opportunity for women's movements is structured differently, even within the same institution, depending upon the movement's goals and its internal and external positions vis-à-vis the institution. Most research on women's movements and feminist movements has focused on women's movements positioned externally to institutions and the movement's attempts to exact policy changes.[59]

Beckwith argues that women's movements have political opportunities to act, even though those opportunities are structurally gendered. Space for women to act may open in states experiencing revolution, although such opening of space does not ensure successful mobilization and changes in society and government. She examines the case of East German feminist groups whose divisions were such that they were unable to take advantage of the period of democratization in East Germany and the reunification with West Germany in the early 1990s. In the end they were cut off and "disempowered."[60]

While the case of East German feminist groups demonstrates the difficulty in taking advantage of the opening of the political space for women's activism, other cases show that conflict and crisis do provide opportunities for women to move from the private to public sphere through their participation in women's movements. As scholars have noted, many women participate in such movements by stressing their roles as wives and mothers; Elissa Helms remarks women are "keepers of the domestic sphere, which reflects their positions in the male-dominated gender-regimes."[61] As Patricia Campbell observes, for a nationalist and/or revolutionary movement to succeed in obtaining its goals of liberation/self-determination, women are needed in the public sphere. The nationalist/revolutionary movements, while dominated by men, will advocate for "gender specific interests."[62] Moreover, a maternal identity enables women to transcend international borders, as Swanee Hunt and Cristina Posa note. With an identity that transcends borders, women are able to find common ground on means to promote peace, particularly a peace that will benefit their communities. Hunt and Posa assert, "And since women know their communities, they can predict acceptance of peace initiatives as well as broker agreements in their own neighborhoods."[63]

The problem for maintaining that momentum emerges when the crisis or conflict ends. Women are expected to retreat from the public sphere and return to the private sphere. With this retreat, gender interests are also placed lower on the list of priorities for the new government.[64] Consequently, feminist scholars such as Tickner caution that women's movements focused on peace that utilize maternal images for their message "may have had some success, [but] they do nothing to change existing gender relations; this allows men to remain in control and continue to dominate the agenda of world politics, and it continues to render women's voices as inauthentic in matters of foreign policymaking."[65] In the chapters that follow, we will see how and whether women's movements, defined as either traditional/essentialist or feminist, are able to obtain their goals and transform their societies, particularly societies and states in conflict.

Women, Conflict, and Political Activism

It is clear that women are affected by conflict at every stage, from pre-conflict through the actual outbreak of violence and into resolving the conflict. Often the roles that women either play, or are placed into, prior to or during a conflict will have a direct impact on the options available to them after the conflict ends. In addressing issues of conflict and security, we can draw on the perspectives of *both* traditional IR theory and feminist IR in the belief that each has something to contribute. Furthermore, we think that both these approaches can complement one another and so we take as our starting point the idea that each can help us understand the stages of conflict and the roles that women play.

In this book it is certainly not possible or viable to focus on all wars or conflicts that have occurred since the end of the Cold War, let alone all those that occurred prior to the contemporary period. In fact, our focus is less on the specific conflicts than on focusing on and understanding women's political activism at various stages in any conflict, from pre-conflict through the outbreak of political violence, to the peace negotiations or resolution of the conflict, and after. Our focus will be on societies in conflict, which may be overt, such as the case of former Yugoslavia or the decade-long war in El Salvador, or on states that are divided, such as South Africa under apartheid, where women played a pivotal role in affecting the reconciliation process. In determining which examples to look at, we focus on cases of "lethal intergroup violence," and, in so doing, support Cockburn's assertion about ethnic and religious conflicts that "these apparently ethnic wars are, in a sense, gender wars. As well as defining a relation between peoples and land, they shape a certain relation between women and men."[66]

It is our contention that women will take political action at each of these stages, although different types of actions depending on the conflict, their perception of security, the options available to them, who they are or can work with, as well as a host of other variables. Furthermore, women's political activism is premised on the need to arrive at or work with other women (and often men as well) in the belief that little will be accomplished unless there is a critical mass willing to fight to make its voices heard.[67]

Just as we can identify a progression along which states move from peace to conflict or war, so there is a range of possible actions that women can take at these various stages from doing nothing to becoming actively engaged with the political process. Those actions can be based on a traditional "motherist" position or may be overtly feminist. Our focus is to apply a gender analysis of women's roles before, during, and after conflict. In doing so, it is important to us to try to understand what particular action or actions women did engage in, why they chose that option or options, and what impact doing so had on the desired outcome, whether that was to avert war or to resolve a conflict. All of these variables—type and stage of conflict, the options available to women and the choices that they made, and the outcomes of those actions—are discussed in more detail in the following chapters.

Notes

[1] See Pnina Werbner and Nira Yuval-Davis, eds. *Women, Citizenship, and Difference* (London: Zed Books, 1999). See also V. Spike Peterson, "Gendered Nationalism": Reproducing

'Us' versus 'Them,'" in *The Women and War Reader*, ed. Lois Ann Lorentzen and Jennifer Turpin, 41–49 (New York: New York University Press, 1998).

[2] Ayala Emmett, *Our Sisters' Promised Land: Women, Politics, and Israeli-Palestinian Coexistence* (Ann Arbor: University of Michigan Press, 2003), 36.

[3] Peterson, "Gendered Nationalism," 43.

[4] Cynthia Cockburn, *The Space between Us: Negotiating Gender and National Identities in Conflict* (London: Zed Books, 1998), 42.

[5] V. Spike Peterson, "Sexing Political Identities/Nationalism as Heterosexism," *International Feminist Journal of Politics* 1, no. 1 (1999): 44.

[6] Ibid., 47.

[7] Peterson, "Gendered Nationalism," 45; idem, "Sexing Political Identities," 51.

[8] Tsjeard Bouta, Georg Frerks, and Ian Bannon, *Gender, Conflict, and Development* (Washington DC: World Bank, 2004), 51.

[9] For a traditional discussion of "levels of analysis" and international relations, see J. David Singer, "The Level-of-Analysis Problem in International Relations," *World Politics*, 14, no. 1 (October 1961): 77–92. Also see Kenneth N. Waltz, *Man, the State, and War: A Theoretical Analysis* (New York: Columbia University Press, 1959).

[10] J. Ann Tickner, *Gendering World Politics: Issues and Approaches in the Post–Cold War Era* (New York: Columbia University Press, 2001), 48–49.

[11] K. J. Holsti, *International Relations: A Framework for Analysis*, 7th ed. (Englewood Cliffs, NJ: Prentice Hall, 1995), 46.

[12] Ibid., 47.

[13] Charles Tilly, *Coercion, Capital, and European States; AD 990–1992* (Cambridge, MA: Blackwell Publishers, 1992), 26.

[14] Tickner, *Gendering World Politics*, 57.

[15] Ibid., 21.

[16] Ibid., 54.

[17] Gillian Youngs, "Feminist International Relations: A Contradiction in Terms? Or: Why Women and Gender Are Essential to Understanding the World 'We' Live In," *International Affairs* 80, no. 1 (2004): 81.

[18] V. Spike Peterson and Anne Sisson Runyan, *Global Gender Issues*, 2nd ed. (Boulder, CO: Westview Press, 1999), 48.

[19] Ibid., 48–49.

[20] Hans J. Morgenthau, *Politics among Nations: The Struggle for Power and Peace*, rev. Kenneth W. Thompson (Boston: McGraw Hill, 1993), 37.

[21] Ibid., 11.

[22] Peterson and Runyan, *Global Gender Issues*, 69.

[23] For an excellent discussion of hard and soft power, and the role of each since the Cold War, see Joseph Nye, *The Paradox of American Power: Why the World's Only Superpower Can't Go It Alone* (New York: Oxford University Press, 2002).

[24] Moregnthau, *Politics among Nations*, 5.

[25] Waltz, *Man, the State, and War*, 35.

[26] Ibid., 47.

[27] J. Cohen, "Women in Peace and War," in *Psychological Factors of Peace and War,* ed. Tom Hatherly Pear (Freeport, NY: Books for Libraries Press, 1971), 93–94.

[28] Waltz, *Man, the State, and War,* 47.

[29] J. Ann Tickner, *Gender in International Relations: Feminist Perspectives on Achieving Global Security* (New York: Columbia University Press, 1992), 29–30.

[30] Joshua S. Goldstein, *War and Gender: How Gender Shapes the War System and Vice Versa* (Cambridge, UK: Cambridge University Press, 2001), 2.

[31] Ibid., 3.

[32] Peterson and Runyan, *Global Gender Issues.*

[33] Morgenthau, *Politics among Nations,* 29.

[34] Barry Hughes, *Continuity and Change in World Politics: The Clash of Perspectives,* 2nd ed. (Englewood Cliffs, NJ: Prentice Hall, 1994), 79.

[35] For more on human security as it relates to state security, see United Nations Office for the Coordination of Humanitarian Affairs (OCHA), "Human Security" (2007). http://ochaonline.un.org/Home/tabid/2097/Default.aspx.

[36] Inger Skjelsbaek, "Gendered Battlefield: A Gender Analysis of Peace and Conflict" (Oslo, Norway: International Peace Research Institute, October 1997), 18. Available online.

[37] Ibid., 19.

[38] Ibid., 3.

[39] Youngs, "Feminist International Relations," 83.

[40] Peterson and Runyan, *Global Gender Issues,* 49.

[41] Ruth Jacobson, Susie Jacobs, and Jennifer Marchbank, "Introduction: States of Conflict," in *States of Conflict: Gender, Violence and Resistance,* ed. Susie Jacobs, Ruth Jacobson, and Jennifer Marchbank (London: Zed Books, 2000), 4.

[42] Donna Pankhurst, "Women, Gender, and Peacebuilding," Working Paper 5, Center for Conflict Resolution (Bradford UK: University of Bradford, August 2000), 7.

[43] Tickner, *Gender in International Relations,* 58. This relationship is stressed by Cynthia Cockburn in *The Space between Us,* and is a relationship noted by others as well. See, for example, Laurence McKeown and Simona Sharoni, "Formations and Transformations of Masculinity in the North of Ireland and in Israel-Palestine," unpublished paper (2002); and also Kaufman and Williams, *Women, the State, and War,* 173–74, which summarizes our findings on this issue.

[44] Johann Galtung, "Violence, Peace, and Peace Research," *Journal of Peace Research* 6, no. 3 (1969): 171.

[45] Cynthia Cockburn, *From Where We Stand: War, Women's Activism and Feminist Analysis* (London: Zed Books, 2007), 190–91.

[46] Karen Beckwith and Kimberley Cowell-Meyers, "Sheer Numbers: Critical Representation Thresholds and Women's Political Representation," *Perspectives on Politics* 5, no. 3 (September 2007): 554.

[47] Ibid., 554.

[48] Ibid., 556.

[49] Ibid., 557.

[50] Ibid., 558.

[51] Ibid, 559.

[52] Karen Beckwith, "The Comparative Politics of Women's Movements," *Perspectives on Politics* 3, no. 3 (September 2005): 589–90.

[53] Karen Beckwith, "Beyond Compare? Women's Movements in Comparative Perspective," *European Journal of Political Research* 37 (2000): 436.

[54] Ibid., 437–38.

[55] Beckwith, "The Comparative Politics of Women's Movements," 585.

[56] Beckwith, "Beyond Compare?" 437.

[57] Ibid., 441. For an overview of ZEST, see Cynthia Cockburn, "A Women's Political Party for Yugoslavia: Introduction to the Serbian Feminist Manifesto," *Feminist Review* 39 (Winter 1991): 155–60.

[58] Beckwith, "Beyond Compare?" 452.

[59] Ibid., 446–47.

[60] Ibid., 448–49.

[61] Elissa Helms, "Gender Essentialisms and Women's Activism in Post-War Bosnia-Herzegovina," in *Feminists under Fire: Exchanges across War Zones*, ed. Wenona Giles et al. (Toronto: Between the Lines, 2003), 181.

[62] Patricia J. Campbell, "Gender and Post-Conflict Civil Society," *International Feminist Journal of Politics* 7, no. 3 (September 2005): 377–78.

[63] Swanee Hunt and Cristina Posa, "Women Waging Peace," *Foreign Policy* 124 (May-June 2001): 41.

[64] Campbell, "Gender and Post-Conflict Civil Society," 377–78.

[65] Tickner, *Gendering World Politics*, 60.

[66] Cockburn, *The Space between Us*, 13.

[67] In her report Skjelsbaek writes: "The Danish political scientist Drude Dahlerup has conducted several studies of the impact of the increase in women's participation in Scandinavian politics. Her point of departure is that women in themselves cannot make a difference unless they constitute a *critical mass*—a concept from nuclear physics that refers to the quantity needed to start a chain reaction" (Skjelsbaek, "Gendered Battlefields," 19).

Chapter 3

Conflict and Violence Against Women

In the previous chapter we laid out the theoretical framework that included our understanding and definitions of critical concepts such as war, conflict, and security as drawn from and tied to the IR literature. What is striking are the ways in which the changing nature of warfare have had a direct impact on women, often engaging them in the conflicts and making them victims of acts of violence simply because of their ethnic, religious, or tribal affiliations, or in some cases, even more insidiously, simply because they happened to be in the wrong place at the wrong time. In some cases this means that women had to make choices—to fight, to flee, or to remain and face the consequences. Even though they were often excluded from the initial decisions to engage in the conflict, they clearly were affected by those decisions. Ultimately, as we argue here, among the decisions that women make are whether to engage in some kind of political action, what type of actions, and when to do so. In making the decisions to take action of some kind, women gain power and agency in the face of often dire circumstances. The decisions that women make to engage in political action are not exclusive of the other sets of decisions that they have to make (fight, flee, or remain) but are in fact often related because one set of actions directly affect another.

The idea of conflict affecting women is not new; the violence that is associated with conflict and war has long affected women, often in ways that make them relatively powerless to respond. There are countless historical examples going back to ancient Greek and Roman times citing cases where women were abducted and raped because they were seen as spoils of war. However, what has changed has been the public attention given to the perpetration of violence against women during situations of conflict, and the apparent lack of, or minimal response to, these acts by the international community because of the sanctity of the sovereign state. Vocal outcry can lead to public statements condemning such acts but are virtually meaningless without corresponding action—either political or military—to address the situation, to bring to justice those who committed them, or to protect those who are most vulnerable, that is, the women and children.

Jennifer Turpin states that "war has profound and unique effects on women." And she also documents the ways in which recent wars have been especially severe in their effects on women due, in part, to "the development of increasingly efficient war-making technologies that make war and militarism more deadly." She also notes that civilians are the majority of those killed in war, and of those numbers of civilians killed "the vast majority" are women and children.[1] Thus, while men are also affected by war and conflict, women are especially vulnerable not only as civilians but because they are susceptible to sexual violence that is perpetrated not only by adversaries, but sometimes by the guards who are supposed to protect them. Even in refugee camps where women go or are placed in order to escape the conflict, they are not immune to acts of violence. In fact, the very act of fleeing violence can become dangerous and threatening rather than an act of sanctuary.

As Turpin and others also stress, the causes of the violence against women during conflict are not only militarily inflicted. In fact, there is a direct correlation between an increase in domestic violence and conflict; incidences of domestic violence increase during conflict, when militarization becomes the social norm. The literature supports this correlation between a militarized society and domestic violence, which clearly affects women the most.[2] But as Turpin also makes clear, just as the wars and conflict zones seem to be concentrated in the so-called developing world, so too the women who are most vulnerable will vary by geographic location even within a war-torn country, economic (and by implication educational) status, and racial and ethnic identity. Furthermore, the disruptions caused by conflict that affect women are not only in the area of physical violence. Rather, women are more likely to be uprooted by war, either by choice or by force, and become refugees (internally displaced people within their country or refugees crossing state territorial boundaries), which brings its own set of problems and issues.

This chapter explores specifically some of the ways in which conflict and war affect women directly as a way of setting the stage for understanding women's possible responses to this situation at various points from the early onset of conflict, during the conflict, and in preparing for a post-conflict society. We focus on the primary ways in which women are violated, either literally or figuratively, during situations of conflict, that is, rape and displacement. Both of these inflict harm on women who were not directly involved with the decisions to go to war or engage in conflict, but were nonetheless affected by those decisions in a way that altered their existence significantly.

In the approach we are taking here it is important to understand the ways in which women are affected by conflict (physically, emotionally, psychologically, and politically), in order to get a better understanding of the options open to them as they determine how to respond to the situations they face. Implicit in this is our assumption that although they had little input into the initial decisions to engage in war and conflict, women can and do make choices about the situations that they are forced to confront as a result of the decisions made by others. Much has been written about violence against women during times of conflict, and the documentation is indeed gruesome. What is clear in the literature is that while the actual conflicts might vary—the countries, the reasons for the conflicts, the combatants— there are similarities across virtually all modern conflicts in the ways in which women are affected. Identifying these similarities will provide the backdrop for understanding women's choices in responding.

Gendering Armed Conflict: Rape and Sexual Violence as Strategic Instruments of War

It is considered a truism that during war and conflict both rape and sexual violence "are as old a practice as war itself." At the same time, rape and sexual violence have not been evident in considerations of international humanitarian law.[3] This observation carries within it two important points that we explore here: first, that rape and sexual violence are a given in conflict situations. This is neither new nor startling, but it is important to explore nonetheless. The second point derives directly from the first, and that is the scant attention given to this set of crimes within the purview of international law until recently. It is virtually impossible to address one piece without looking at the other.

Rape and Sexual Violence

One of the basic tenets of conflict and the attendant violence directed at civilians that goes with it is the need to identify and isolate the "other," specifically the group that becomes the enemy. In their primarily anthropological study of the wars in Yugoslavia, Joel Halpern and David Kideckel note that "those responsible for political decision-making lead societies where the definition of a desired future is based on an idealized past of one's own group. This is often strengthened by simultaneously demonizing the 'Other,' whether that Other is the former secular, multinational state, the 'religious/national' groups in now-neighboring states, or even dissident groups within one's own nation."[4] Violating women sexually is one way to assert domination over the "other" in the most humiliating way possible. This is a pattern that can be seen repeatedly in both past and recent conflicts. For example, during the independence movement in Bangladesh in 1971 violence was widespread.

In her study of women and conflict in South Asia, Anuradha Chenoy notes: "Besides large-scale genocide, gendered crime was a common feature of these events.

Rape was a frequent form of meting out humiliation to the 'other' community."[5] A heavily Muslim nation, the violation of women in Bangladesh was an extreme form of dishonor that often led to further suffering by their families, who did not know how to endure the violation. The rapes were sometimes carried out by members of informal militias and other times by the soldiers fighting on behalf of a government. For example, during the fighting to prevent Bangladesh from becoming independent, Pakistani soldiers "terrorized the Bengali people with night raids during which women were raped in their villages or carted off to soldiers' barracks."[6]

Subsequent inquiries from the International Court of Justice "revealed that an entire generation of Bengali women was raped or forced into prostitution. [But] once the state was established, it concerned itself with the rehabilitation of *men* and duties of nationhood. Old patterns of gender biases and patriarchy were resumed" (emphasis added).[7] This supports the contentions noted above not only about the role that rape played, but also about the inability or unwillingness of the international system of justice to address the violence against women as an ongoing part of humanitarian law.

These same patterns were played out in many other cases where rape and sexual violence were part of the strategic weapons used by one side against the other. As Coomaraswamy documents, "The recent wars in Bosnia-Herzegovina, Rwanda and Kosovo point to the fact that sexual violence can be a central instrument of terror especially in campaigns that involve fratricide or nationalist wars." She continues, "Rape and sexual violence have been used to assert dominance over one's enemy. Since women's sexuality is seen as being under the protection of the men of the community, its defilement is an act of domination over the males of the community or group that is under attack."[8] Rape and sexual violence are very much "public" acts, given that the humiliation and violence women experience are "witnessed by others in their community."[9] There are countless other recent examples, such as Somalia and Sudan, where the same patterns of sexual violence against women were used to define the "other," show dominance over a group, and humiliate the men, not to mention the impact that it obviously had on the women who were brutally violated. Sexual violence is used for several purposes, according to Michele L. Leiby, as demonstrated in her study of sexual violence in Guatemala and Peru in wartime. Sexual violence, sanctioned or known by the Peruvian state, occurred against women of suspected or actual guerrilla groups opposed to the state. In that case the state failed to act to protect women from "the widespread sexual violence." In the case of Guatemala, Leiby argues that sexual violence "was an explicit tool of repression, employed indiscriminately against the indigenous peasantry. Victims were not punished for joining the insurgency. Victims were not interrogated for information. Instead, sexual violence was used to spread fear and terror throughout entire 'communities of interest.'"[10] Moreover, sexual violence and rape by men has a performative function. In the case of gang rape, according to Miranda Alison, groups of men bond, in essence contributing to "a sense of loyalty between men." Men who would otherwise not rape women as an individual act of violence "do rape collectively in a group assertion of masculinity."[11] Thus assault on women is indeed a strategic tool of war, one that has become increasingly common.

Rape, therefore, takes on important symbolic meanings tied to the gendered perspective of the state. As noted in Chapter 2, women and motherhood are important symbolic markers within the nation. The work of Nira Yuval-Davis and Floya Anthias, Pnina Werbner, and also V. Spike Peterson identifies the critical markers of "gendered nationalism," including the ways in which women become the "symbolic markers of the nation and group identity."[12] Thus, rape in time of conflict afflicts symbolic damage to the nation/ethnic group by violating the group identity in the most primal form. According to Coomaraswamy, rape and sexual violence "are also used in ethnic wars to 'pollute' and 'defile' the other side."[13] Women's honor, as well as that of their families (and ethnic/national group), is affected by rape and sexual violence. Thus, most women are unwilling to report incidents of rape and sexual violence. Liz Kelly argues that in remaining silent, women "are exercising agency" in the case of the former Yugoslavia. Recognizing the threat to family honor, women *choose* not to speak out.[14]

The use of rape in wartime also reinforces the domination of men over women in general, and one group of men over another (this also takes into account sexual violence against men and boys of the "other" group as well). In looking at "the social and political aims of rape and sexual violence against women" in cases of ethnic/nationalist conflicts, Giles and Hyndman note two views: "First, violated women are represented as symbols of male power and conquest. . . . Second, violations against women contribute to the demasculinization of conquered men, a symbolic process where some men are labeled as 'incompetent.'"[15] Or, as Copelon describes the relationship, women "are targets because they too *are* the enemy, because of their power as well as vulnerability as women, including their sexual and reproductive power." Women are also considered targets "because of *hatred* of their power as women; because of endemic objectification of women; because rape embodies male domination and female subordination" (emphasis in original).[16] And, although Copelon did not say it, because of women's relative powerlessness to fight back.

In a recent study Maria Eriksson Baaz and Maria Stern conducted interviews with soldiers in the Congo (DRC) who had engaged in rape or sexual violence against women. Baaz and Stern found that with the outbreak of war, such gender-based violence became normalized in the communities. Moreover, they found that the sexual violence by civilians increased during the conflict. In the interviews the soldiers explained that while rape and sexual violence are wrong, men have "sexual needs." In this way the soldiers framed their behavior in terms of masculinity and heterosexual manhood.[17]

In addition, women are often targeted for the critical role that they play within society, especially during wartime, when the burden falls to women to hold the society together while, traditionally, the men are fighting. Within a nation at war it is this ability, often born of necessity, that gives women the power they do have. To attack them sexually undermines that power. Thus, rape becomes a war crime of gender where women are targeted for their vulnerability, for the message it sends to their own men as well as to the enemy's men who commit the rapes, and for the symbolism associated with violating women.

Rape and Pregnancy

The fact of rape during conflict is made even more complicated by the issue of pregnancy, which furthers the notion of the domination of one group over another. Rape humiliates women and their families by forcing them to bear a child of the enemy, who then takes the ethnicity of the father rather than the mother. This perverts the notion of motherhood as a symbolic marker by making pregnancy and motherhood a spoil of war. Peterson argues that the "child-bearing capacity" of women "is situated under the control of male-dominated elites, in service to group reproduction through heteropatriarchal family forms and relations."[18] Men use this control during conflict to impregnate women. As Coomaraswamy puts it: "Forced pregnancy is a new aspect that has been recorded in modern wars where racial and ethnic purity are valued."[19] Or, in the words of Thomas and Ralph, "Although rape is a sex-specific type of abuse, it generally functions like other forms of torture to intimidate and punish individual women. In some instances, however, it can also strike a sex-specific function, when, for example, it is committed with the intent of impregnating its victims." Thomas and Ralph quote one Bosnian rape victim, who relayed, "It was their aim to make a baby. They wanted to humiliate us. They would say directly, looking into your eyes, that they wanted to make a baby."[20] In that case the baby that was the result of the rape would be a Serb baby, thereby increasing the violation of the Bosnian (Muslim) women.

Turpin equates mass rape and genocide when she claims that "genocide could be accomplished by the mass rape of women of the enemy's ethnic group [that] derives from a patriarchal definition of ethnicity." Because of the connection between the notion that women are considered to be "the symbols of the family" and that the foundation of society is the family unit, "the humiliation for women giving birth to the enemy's children symbolizes the destruction of community."[21]

The use of rape to impregnate women reinforces the humiliation of women and their families while apparently elevating the status of the men who are the violators.

As Copelon remarks, "When examined through a feminist lens, forced pregnancy appears to be an assault on the reproductive self-determination of women; it expresses the desire to mark the rape and the rapist upon the woman's body and upon the woman's life."[22] This can be seen not only in Bosnia, where reports of such violations are legion, but in Rwanda, Sudan, Sri Lanka, and many other cases where ethnic and nationalist violence have raged for years. This takes a toll not only on the mother but on the child conceived out of hatred. Coomaraswamy relates the story of meeting a woman in East Timor who had a child born after a rape by an Indonesian soldier. "She told us how she hated and neglected this child until a counselor and a nun taught her how not to pass on her outrage and anger to an innocent child. The body language of mother and child was plain for the world to see." As she also stresses, in Catholic and Muslim countries, where abortion is either not possible or difficult, many women have little choice but to give birth to these children.[23]

These examples show how women are abused during wartime, with few options at their disposal to resist. However, for some women, the abuses they have to endure can become a source of strength as well as a factor that motivates them to take action. Rather than complying with the will of the enemy, it strengthens their resolve to fight back in some way. Within their households the breakdown of the traditional patriarchal norms under which women had lived forces them to start taking control of their own lives and the lives of their children, out of necessity or choice. For some, that means economic and financial independence, perhaps for the first time. For others, it might mean asserting themselves politically so that they make decisions that allow them to feel empowered. Those options, and the ways in which women choose to become engaged politically, are explored in more detail in the following chapters.

Sexual Violence During Conflict and the International System

We noted above Coomaraswamy's assertion that rape and sexual violence that take place during war and conflict have been "invisible in the discussion of international humanitarian law." We think that this is an important topic for further exploration here, albeit briefly. Are these crimes really "invisible" in international humanitarian laws? But tied to that is another important question: what can and have *women* done to assert their rights against these violations?

Before moving into a broad discussion of the ways in which the international system does—or more often does not—respond to or address these violations, it is important to begin by asking why so little is done to respond to or to stop the violations while they are occurring and why, often despite the lip service that political leaders pay to the heinous nature of the crimes, these same leaders are unwilling to intervene. Part of the reticence of political leaders outside the country to step in and take whatever actions are necessary pertain to the sanctity of sovereignty as a central concept in international law. Holsti notes that although this prohibition has been breached frequently, primarily when it is argued that it is in the national interest of the state to do so, few states are willing to argue that it is in their own national interest to intervene in the cause of stopping human rights abuses, rape, ethnic cleansing, and so forth in countries far away from their own territory.[24] Or, as Thomas and Ralph describe it, "Rape has long been mischaracterized and dismissed by military and political leaders—in other words, those in a position to stop it—as a private crime, a sexual act, the ignoble conduct of the occasional soldier, or, worse still, it has been accepted because it is so commonplace."[25]

What is especially insidious about this selective application of the concept of sovereignty is that it coincides with the increasing use of sexual crimes and other gender-based violations concomitant with an increase in ethnic, religious, and nationalist conflicts. Sellers "argues that the early codes of chivalry were explicit about the prohibition of rape during war time. However, in the nineteenth and twentieth centuries this seems to have disappeared."[26] As a result, crimes and violence against women have become a given in recent intrastate/national conflicts.

If countries and national leaders do not see intervention in rape and other human rights violations as within the national interest, and if human rights groups are relatively powerless to intervene, then it falls to the tenets of international law to become the umbrella under which such violations are addressed. Both The Hague Convention and the 1949 Geneva Convention do speak about "violation of honor," and Article 27 of the Geneva Convention is very explicit regarding the treatment of women:

> Protected persons are entitled, in all circumstances, to respect for their persons, their honor, their family rights, their religious convictions and practices, and their manners and customs. They shall at all times be humanely treated, and shall be protected especially against all acts of violence or threats thereof and against insults and public curiosity. *Women shall be especially protected against any attack on their honor, in particular against rape, enforced prostitution, or any form of indecent assault.* (emphasis added)[27]

But according to Coomaraswamy, both "The Hague Convention and the Geneva Convention speak about the violation of honor, but the Geneva Convention does not explicitly make sexual violence a grave breach that falls under universal jurisdiction and that holds an individual criminally responsible."[28] This means that even under cases when a perpetrator may be caught and tried, it is unlikely that he will be held accountable or responsible for rape as a crime against humanity.

Following the Geneva Convention, not much attention was paid by the international community to the issue of violence against women until the early 1990s. In

December 1993 the United Nations General Assembly adopted Resolution 48/ 104, the UN Declaration on the Elimination of Violence Against Women. The declaration focused on violence against women as a violation of women's human rights, stressing that such violence

> is a manifestation of historically unequal power relations between men and women, which have led to domination over and discrimination against women by men and to the prevention of the full advancement of women, and that violence against women is one of the crucial social mechanisms by which women are forced into a subordinate position compared with men.

The declaration further acknowledges that "women in situations of armed conflict, are especially vulnerable to violence."[29] While the declaration highlighted the issue of violence against women in wartime, it did not declare rape and sexual violence war crimes.

In order to address the apparent failing in international law as regards the Geneva Convention and the scant attention paid to the issue of violence against women since the convention, Coomaraswamy continues, "Due to the vigorous campaigning by women's groups, the new Rome Statute of the International Criminal Court passed in July 2000 makes rape and all forms of sexual violence a war crime and a crime against humanity and ensures that it applies both to external and internal wars."[30] This is one clear example of women working together to influence international law specifically for the protection of women. But it also begs the question of how effectively that international law is enforced, given, once again, that the primary means of enforcement are dominated by men.

In fact, the record shows that most of the prosecution and international legal responses to sexual attacks and violence against women have come in the form of special international tribunals convened to address an individual case. Giles and Hyndman note that "assessment of international responses to gender-specific crimes and evaluations of the place of such crimes in relation to crimes against humanity are crucial to the debates around violence and women's rights." They look at the example of the creation in 1993 of the International Criminal Tribunal for the former Yugoslavia (ICTY) as "an important focus of feminist analysis."[31] According to its website, the ICTY "is a United Nations court of law dealing with war crimes that took place during the conflicts in the Balkans in the 1990's. Since its establishment in 1993 it has irreversibly changed the landscape of international humanitarian law and provided victims an opportunity to voice the horrors they witnessed and experienced." In 1996 the tribunal "issued indictments for the arrest of eight men, charged with sexual assault 'for the purposes of . . . torture and enslavement.' For the first time in history, rape was being prosecuted as a weapon of war and a 'crime against humanity.'"[32]

What was especially important about this ruling, according to Giles and Hyndman, was that although rape and sexual violence have long been a part of war, until this time "these issues have been rendered invisible or incidental because they were dismissed as private acts, the 'aberrational practices of errant soldiers.' The tacit theater of war was the battlefield, the public space around which the rules of war—the Geneva Conventions—had been written. But the public/private divide between the battlefield and people's bodies had dissolved."[33] What this did was to recognize and codify rape as a weapon of war that can—and should—be prosecuted.

According to its website, the International Criminal Tribunal for Rwanda was established in 1994 specifically

> for the prosecution of persons responsible for genocide and other serious violations of international humanitarian law committed in the territory of Rwanda between 1 January 1994 and 31 December 1994. It may also deal with the prosecution of Rwandan citizens responsible for genocide and other such violations of international law committed in the territory of neighboring States during the same period.

Article 3 of the statute specifically makes rape a "crime against humanity" and therefore subject to prosecution and punishment.

While both of these tribunals took important steps in defining rape during wartime as a serious crime that needs to be investigated and punished, they also put violence against women into specific case-based situations rather than within the framework of the broader international criminal court. Nonetheless, in each case the tribunal responded to the need to hold accountable those who committed acts of violence against women during conflict and who acted outside the established rules of war.

With the tribunals firmly establishing sexual violence against women as a war crime, the UN Security Council began to recognize the issue of sexual violence in 2000 as a threat to peace and security, but little was accomplished "to effectively prevent and address such violence." Even with compelling evidence of gender-based violence against women and girls in places such as Sudan and Cote d'Ivorie, according to Human Rights Watch, "the Security Council failed to raise sexual violence at all as an issue of concern."[34] With a series of resolutions, however, the Security Council brought to the forefront the issue of sexual violence and rape as a security concern for the international community. In June 2008 the Security Council unanimously adopted Resolution 1820. With this resolution the Security Council "demanded the 'immediate and complete cessation by all parties to armed conflict of all acts of sexual violence against civilians.'" The resolution stated that "rape and other forms of sexual violence can constitute war crimes, crimes against humanity or a constitutive act with respect to genocide." Further, in attempting to enforce the resolution, the Security Council "affirms its intention, when establishing and renewing state-specific sanctions regimes, to take into consideration the appropriateness of targeted and graduated measures against parties to situations of armed conflict who commit rape and other forms of sexual violence against women and girls in situations of armed conflict."[35]

Resolution 1820 was followed the next year by Resolution 1888, adopted by the Security Council in September 2009. This resolution "signals a robust political commitment to addressing conflict-affected sexual violence as a peace and security issue." Importantly, according to the United Nations Development Fund for Women (UNIFEM), resolution 1888 "provides for an ambitious platform for action, along with high-level leadership in the form of a Special Representative of the Secretary-General on sexual violence in conflict, to ensure UN leadership and coordination to respond to sexual violence."[36]

The United Nations Action Against Sexual Violence in Conflict (UN Action) is a further example of the international community's effort to raise awareness of gender-based violence. The United Nations established UN Action, an inter-agency entity that brings together thirteen UN agencies (such as UNICEF, the World Health Organization, the UN Development Fund for Women, and the United Nations High Commissioner for Refugees) to end sexual violence during and after conflict. Recognizing that sexual violence in wartime and conflict "remains vastly under-addressed due to weak national protection mechanisms, inadequate judicial redress and piecemeal services for survivors," UN Action's creation is a response to calls from NGOs, rape survivors, and women's rights organizations for action at the international community level. This UN entity sets out to "enhance" the various Security Council resolutions (including 1820) that deal with sexual violence against civilians.[37]

Through the resolutions, UN Action, and the creation of the special representative to the secretary-general on sexual violence in conflict, the international community has signaled that sexual violence and rape during conflict are violations of international law, and states and parties to conflict must take action to prevent such gender-based violence. The Security Council resolutions, for example, have made it clear that state-level judicial and legal reforms are necessary to ensure that survivors have adequate access to justice, that civilian and military leaders "demonstrate commitment and political will to prevent sexual violence and to combat impunity and enforce accountability," and that sexual violence issues must be addressed "from the outset of peace processes and mediation efforts, in order to protect populations at risk and promote full stability." In addition, Resolution 1888 and others (such as 1325, which we address more specifically in Chapter 5) recognize the need for women to have a place at the formal peace talks as well as inclusion in peacekeeping missions, given that victims of sexual violence may feel more comfortable reporting abuse to women serving in such missions.[38] With the creation of the position of special representative to the secretary-general on sexual violence in conflict, the UN further demonstrates its commitment to addressing the issue of sexual violence. The first special representative, Margot Wallström of Sweden, was appointed in early 2010. She brings with her the leadership role she played in increasing the awareness of the need to implement UN Security Council Resolutions 1325 and 1820.[39] The special representative's role is "to lead, coordinate, and advocate for efforts to end conflict-related sexual violence against women and children."[40] As Wallström stated, "Sexual violence against women is not cultural, it is criminal, and it is not a women's issue, it is a human rights issue."[41]

In the end, however, the effectiveness of the tribunals and international law to take action is limited by effective implementation and enforcement by the international community as well as the stigma associated with gender-based violence for those women who are the victims. The Security Council has yet to implement Resolution 1888; states in conflict have yet to face targeted sanctions for gender-based violence. Additionally, underlying some of the limitations are questions of whether women, who have already been subjected to so much humiliation and abuse, will be willing to come forward and confront their attackers. Copelon makes the point that

> women are terrified and, at best, reluctant to come forward and charge rape. Admitting rape in a sexist society is a public dishonoring and has consequences for the ability to continue or build relationships with one's community and with male partners. . . . To charge rape is to risk retaliation and death, a risk heightened by war and by knowing and being known to the rapist. To charge rape usually is to risk being raped again—figuratively at least—by the law enforcers.[42]

If the international options of a tribunal or other aspects of international law have failed women in these circumstances, then once again women are put into a position of having to take action, whether by bringing lawsuits against those who violated them, by working together to publicize the situation, or by determining how to exert political pressure on governments to ensure that women's rights are not violated or, when they are, that punishment will be meted out to those who took those actions. In other words, although violated, the women are not silent victims.

Women as Refugees

The impact of conflict situations on women can be seen in any number of other ways as well. Those who chose to flee the violence face another difficult set of circumstances. Yuval-Davis describes the often bifurcated effects of war, which make it especially difficult on women:

> At one extreme, war can have little or hardly any effect if the war is taking place away from the home front, the military involved is professional, and there are few casualties. . . . At the other extreme, most or even all of the determinants of one's daily life and personal identity before the war can disappear in a few hours—place of work, property, homes, personal artifacts, and worst of all, friends, relatives and members of one's family.

She continues that under this latter set of circumstances, "life becomes solely about survival. Many people become refugees in this process, and this is a gendered experience. Up to 80 percent of the total refugee population is composed of women and children."[43]

Cynthia Cockburn notes that war and conflict are not the only causes of the refugee population, as people flee famine, seek asylum, or choose not to return to their country of origin for other reasons. However, the vast majority are displaced by war. She also notes that the disproportionate number of refugees who are women often does not take into account the fact that the men who voluntarily left to join the military or militias were imprisoned or were murdered.[44] Whatever the reasons, it is women who become refugees or internally displaced peoples, and who have to deal with the challenges and often harsh realities that go with that status.

In her study of the impact of war on women in Bosnia, Kosovo, and Afghanistan, Julie A. Mertus states: "In addition to seeking physical protection from violence, a woman imperiled by war seeks assistance in providing adequate food, shelter, health care, and a sense of security to her family."[45] She then enumerates the range of concerns that women often face, "each of which have a gendered aspect." Among these are "lack of protection from violence and other forms of abuse and exploitation"; "depression, despondency, and feelings of hopelessness"; "ruptured human contact"; "inability to find meaningful work"; "lack of access to basic items needed for daily life"; "lack of access to health care and other services"; and "difficulty in extracting legal and administrative remedies."[46]

While fleeing the violence, women can become the victims of sexual attack by marauding militias who take advantage of the women's vulnerabilities. And as refugees, the women become vulnerable in other ways. For example, in the case of Somali refugees, "those who leave the camps in search of fuel with which to cook—predominantly women and girls—are at risk of being attacked."[47] In Darfur, Sudan, in a four-month period (October 2004–February 2005), Médecins Sans Frontières (Doctors Without Borders) treated roughly five hundred displaced women for rape. "More than 80 percent of the rapes occurred when women left in search of water, firewood or grass for animal fodder."[48] Moreover, sexual extortion of refugee women for safe passage, relief supplies, documents, and refugee status further victimizes women.[49] Thus, the refugee camps, while providing one of the few areas of protection, can be, or can become, conflict zones in and of themselves.

Few would argue about the importance of the work done by the United Nations High Commission for Refugees (UNHCR), which "has a mandate to respond to crises of human displacement on a global scale." Although Hyndman maintains that the ways in which the UNHCR "conceives of gender and culture in this humanitarian context invite analysis because of its tendency either to essentialize 'women' and 'culture' in the planning process or to efface the importance of differences vis-à-vis gender policies that focus on integration," she also acknowledges that "shortcomings of humanitarian aid and its delivery in acute situations are generally outweighed by a political consensus that humanitarian action must be taken."[50] Nonetheless, women in refugee situations face a range of possible problems and issues.

At the same time, women in refugee camps often create "a sense of community," according to Meintjes, Pillay, and Tershen, which in turn leads to the creation of "new identities and relationships, in the camps." Importantly, the new identities, relationships and sense of community lead to a recognition by these women that they have human rights, rights that are protected under international law. The authors note that "such new ideas are important in changing relationships between women and men."[51] The experience women have living in refugee camps also gives women an example for leadership in the post-conflict period "because many women become agents of change" while in those camps. Meintjes, Pillay, and Tershen caution, however, that not all refugee camps afford such leadership skill opportunities.[52]

Further contributing to the difficulties women face in times of war and conflict are those in which women seek formal asylum. As Heaven Crawley points out, the violence women experience both within the family unit and the community "has typically been considered outside the realm of international refugee law." Given that this kind of violence is considered within the private sphere, and not the public sphere, international law has not adequately addressed these women's needs for protection.[53] Consequently, when women do seek refugee status and protection, they are unlikely to report the violence due to fears of ostracism from the community and family. Crawley notes that the difficulty arises in demonstrating that the claims of rape and sexual violence are credible. Even when the claims are deemed credible, women face further difficulty in demonstrating that the state did not protect them. Again, the view is that what happens in the home and community are private matters, not matters for the state—the public sphere.[54] She makes the point that "a feminist reconceptualization of the role and legal understanding of rape and war involves recognizing the use of rape and sexual violence by the state or by parties that the state is unable or unwilling to control during armed conflict."[55]

The international community has been slow to acknowledge that women refugees need protection. The 1951 Geneva Convention relating to the Status of Refugees defines a refugee as one who

as a result of events occurring before 1 January 1951 and owing to well-founded fear of being persecuted for reasons of race, religion, nationality, membership of a particular social group or political opinion, is outside the country of his nationality and is unable or, owing to such fear, is unwilling to avail himself of the protection of that country; or who, not having a nationality and being outside the country of his former habitual residence as a result of such events, is unable or, owing to such fear, is unwilling to return to it.

This definition does not mention gender or sex, or that women may be persecuted by virtue of the fact that they are women (the definition also uses the masculine pronoun *he* throughout).

Only in the past decade or so has the international community attempted to address women as a special category in need of refugee status and protection. For example, in 1991 the UNHCR produced *Guidelines on the Protection of Refugee Women*, which called on states to consider giving women refugee status if they could be persecuted "for violating social norms." (In 2008 the document was replaced by the UNHCR Handbook for the Protection of Women and Girls, which further highlighted the issue affecting refugee women and girls, and the role the international community and individual states can play in addressing those issues.) Freedman points out that states may be reluctant to consider women a "particular social group," however, due to fears that there would be a significant increase in asylum claims by women.[56]

As Human Rights Watch points out, the UNHCR has only recently "begun to focus on the need to address the issue of rape and other forms of sexual assault against refugee women." These women face the threat of sexual violence while fleeing as well as when they become refugees. Once they arrive in the host country, "women refugees are targeted for rape because they are refugees, because of their actual or perceived political or ethnic affiliations, and because they are women." While the UNHCR has policies to help women who have experienced sexual violence, these policies are not well integrated into existing "UNHCR programs and services in the field." The exceptions are the Vulnerable Women and Children's Programme in Somali refugee camps located in Kenya.[57] In issuing *Sexual Violence Against Refugees: Guidelines on the Prevention and Response* document in 1995 (the document was updated in 2003), the UNHCR recognized specifically the issue of sexual violence against women refugees and measures to prevent sexual violence. In addition, the agency created the post of senior coordinator for refugee women, based in Geneva, as well as "regional coordinators on women's issues."[58] Human Rights Watch claims, however, that the documents noted above "are often overlooked or deliberately ignored by UNHCR staff," due to unawareness or lack of knowledge of the contents of the documents, the massive numbers of refugees that need to be processed and administered to, and so forth. There is no system in place that activates an automatic response from either those in the branch offices or headquarters in Geneva to make sure that the personnel with the training and expertise in the area of sexual violence against women are sent to the location where the violence is occurring to deal with the matter expeditiously.[59]

As different cases have shown, trying to meet those challenges can also lead to increased politicization and activism on the part of those women. For example, the violence women experience has led women to organize within states as well as across them to attempt to change asylum processes to include gender. In fact, in the United States, Australia, and Canada, women's activism has led to these countries recognizing that gender needs to be taken into account during the process for asylum.[60] In another example, the UNHCR hosted a conference, Dialogue with Refugee Women, in June 2001 that brought together more than fifty refugee women and UNHCR staff (prior to the conference, regional and local consultations were held, involving more than five hundred refugee women, NGOs, UNHCR staff, and host states). During this two-day conference, refugee women were given a voice, telling the UNHCR what needed to be done to help refugee women and men.[61] The report on the conference notes that the issues that the refugee women focused on are not new; rather, the issues are the same ones that were noted at the first International Consultation on Refugee Women in 1988. These issues include the protection of refugee women whether they are living in refugee camps, urban or rural areas, or returning. General insecurity as well as the specific insecurity that comes from sexual and gender-based violence remains a problem. As the report notes, "Stigma and the generalized impunity of those who carry out the violence prevent women from speaking out."[62]

In addition to the issue of protecting refugee women, other issues include the need for land and property rights, access to education at all levels, mechanisms to acquire an income, projects to develop skills, promotion of the consultation of refugee women, improvement of the participation of refugee women in UNHCR decision-making as well as decision-making in other leadership roles (including the involvement of women in peace initiatives), and the inclusion of men in the process to promote and ensure the equal rights of these women.[63] The refugee women made clear the complexity of their situation: they are economically, politically, and socially vulnerable due to the pervasive gendering of their situation. As heads of household if their husbands, fathers, or brothers are no longer living with them (perhaps due to the fact that they are fighting or have been killed) or if the men are living in the home but unable to find work, women face challenges of finding adequate employment. As refugees they often do not have permission from the host country to work, further exacerbating an already difficult situation. When women are dependent on the male family members, women are also insecure. For example, food ration cards are often given to the men, as heads of household, who do not then provide those cards to their spouses and children, and thus women have no access to food. In another example, host countries often provide documentation to men but not the women, thereby restricting women's freedom of movement. Providing documentation only to men rather than each individual can lead to the separation of the family and women's increased dependence on the male members of the family.[64] The refugee women consistently asserted the need for women to have a significant role in the planning and implementation of policies to improve their situation as refugees. As Augusta, a Sierra Leone returnee woman remarked, "We should not ask UNHCR to give us fish. We should rather ask them to show us how to catch fish, so that we can be self-reliant."[65]

The above discussion illustrates the challenges women face as refugees responding to conflict and war. While the UNHCR has taken a more active role (as demonstrated by the various documents and reports issued by the agency) and some UN Security Council Resolutions (1325, 1820) make mention of refugee women, women continue to suffer. They suffer economically when they do not have opportunities for employment to provide for their families, thereby facing the threat of sexual abuse and exploitation. Even when they do have jobs, as the Women's Refugee Commission makes clear, they may suffer domestic violence from the male members of the family who resent the women's ability to access and control those resources.[66] They suffer politically when they do not have access to documentation necessary for the asylum determination process and when they do not have access to decision-making in terms of planning and implementing policies that would improve their situation. And they suffer physically when they are the victims of sexual violence, rape, gender-based violence, forced impregnation, and so forth because of their ethnic, political, or religious identity, or because they are women.

Conclusion

There is little doubt that the intrastate conflicts and wars—whether ethnic, nationalist, or religious—that have proliferated since the end of the Cold War (with many having started during the Cold War) have had a profound effect on women. Furthermore, it is also clear that the international community is either ill-prepared or unwilling to take significant actions on behalf of those women. This chapter documents some of the ways in which women in particular were affected by those wars:

sexual attacks, forced bearing of children conceived through rape, displacement, and resettlement. According to Mary Caprioli and Kimberly Lynn Douglass, "Violence against women is related to broader cultural norms permissive of gendered violence, which escalates during conflict." When the conflict ends, the "heightened level of violence often becomes the new norm post-conflict."[67] In this chapter our primary focus was on acts of violence perpetrated against women civilians. Our goal here was to outline some (but not all) of the ways in which war affects women in order to set the stage for women's political responses, which will be developed in more detail in Chapter 4 and Chapter 5.

Notes

[1] Jennifer Turpin, "Many Faces: Women Confronting War," in *The Women and War Reader*, ed. Lois Ann Lorentzen and Jennifer Turpin (New York: New York University Press, 1998), 3–4.

[2] Turpin, "Many Faces." See also, for example, J. Ann Tickner, *Gender in International Relations: Feminist Perspectives on Achieving Global Security* (New York: Columbia University Press, 1992); Cynthia Cockburn, *The Space between Us: Negotiating Gender and National Identities in Conflict* (London: Zed Books, 1998); Laurence McKeown and Simona Sharoni, "Formations and Transformations of Masculinity in the North of Ireland and in Israel-Palestine," unpublished paper (2002); and Joyce P. Kaufman and Kristen P. Williams, *Women, the State, and War* (Lanham, MD: Lexington, 2007), 173–74.

[3] Radhika Coomaraswamy, "A Question of Honour: Women, Ethnicity, and Armed Conflict," in *Feminists under Fire: Exchanges across War Zones*, ed. Wenona Giles, et al. (Toronto: Between the Lines, 2003), 92.

[4] Joel M. Halpern and David A. Kideckel, "Introduction: The End of Yugoslavia Observed," in *Neighbors at War: Anthropological Perspectives on Yugoslav Ethnicity, Culture, and History*, ed. Joel M. Halpern and David A. Kideckel (University Park: The Pennsylvania State University Press, 2000), 4.

[5] Anuradha M. Chenoy, "Militarization, Conflict, and Women in South Asia," in Lorentzen and Turpin, *The Women and War Reader*, 102.

[6] Dorothy Q. Thomas and Regan E. Ralph, "Rape in War: The Case of Bosnia," in *Gender Politics in the Western Balkans: Women and Society in Yugoslavia and the Yugoslav Successor States*, ed. Sabrina P. Ramet, 203–18 (University Park: The Pennsylvania State University Press, 1999), 204.

[7] Chenoy, "Militarization, Conflict, and Women in South Asia," 104.

[8] Coomaraswamy, "A Question of Honour," 92.

[9] Liz Kelly, "Wars against Women: Sexual Violence, Sexual Politics and the Militarized State," in *States of Conflict: Gender, Violence and Resistance*, ed. Susie Jacobs, Ruth Jacobson, and Jennifer Marchbank, 45–65 (London: Zed Books, 2000), 60.

[10] Michele L. Leiby, "Wartime Sexual Violence in Guatemala and Peru," *International Studies Quarterly* 53 (2009): 465–66.

[11] Miranda Alison, "Wartime Sexual Violence: Women's Human Rights and Questions of Masculinity," *Review of International Studies* 33 (2007): 77.

[12] V. Spike Peterson, "Gendered Nationalism: Reproducing 'Us' versus 'Them,'" in Lorentzen and Turpin, *The Women and War Reader*, 44. See also Pnina Werbner and Nira Yuval-Davis, eds. *Women, Citizenship, and Difference* (London: Zed Books, 1999).

[13] Coomaraswamy, "A Question of Honour," 92.

[14] Kelly, "Wars against Women," 53.

[15] Wenona Giles and Jennifer Hyndman, "New Directions for Feminist Research and Politics," in *Sites of Violence: Gender and Conflict Zones*, ed. Wenona Giles and Jennifer Hyndman (Berkeley and Los Angeles: University of California Press, 2004), 309.

[16] Rhonda Copelon, "Surfacing Gender: Reconceptualizing Crimes Against Women in Time of War," in Lorentzen and Turpin, *The Women and War Reader*, 71.

[17] Maria Eriksson Baaz and Maria Stern, "Why Do Soldiers Rape? Masculinity, Violence and Sexuality in the Armed Forces in the Congo (DRC)," *International Studies Quarterly* 53 (2009): 503, 505, 512.

[18] V. Spike Peterson, "Sexing Political Identities/Nationalism as Heterosexism," *International Feminist Journal of Politics* 1, no. 1 (1999): 52.

[19] Coomaraswamy, "A Question of Honour," 92.

[20] Thomas and Ralph, "Rape in War," 208.

[21] Turpin, "Many Faces," 5.

[22] Copelon, "Surfacing Gender," 71.

[23] Coomaraswamy, "A Question of Honour," 95.

[24] K. J. Holsti, *International Relations: A Framework for Analysis*, 7th ed. *(Englewood Cliffs, NJ: Prentice Hall, 1995), 46.

[25] Thomas and Ralph, "Rape in War," 206.

[26] Patricia Sellers, cited in Coomaraswamy, "A Question of Honour," 99.

[27] Part III, Article 27, "Geneva Convention relative to the Protection of Civilian Persons in Time of War Adopted on 12 August 1949 by the Diplomatic Conference for the Establishment of International Conventions for the Protection of Victims of War, held in Geneva from 21 April to 12 August 1949, entry into force 21 October 1950." Available on the www.unhchr.ch website.

[28] Coomaraswamy, "A Question of Honour," 99.

[29] United Nations General Assembly, *Declaration on the Elimination of Violence against Women*, A/RES/48/104 (December 20, 1993).

[30] Coomaraswamy, "A Question of Honour," 99.

[31] Giles and Hyndman, "New Directions," 309.

[32] Ibid.

[33] Ibid.

[34] Human Rights Watch, "UN: Take Action against Rape in War" (May 25, 2008). Available on the www.hrw.org website.

[35] United Nations Security Council, "Security Council Demands Immediate and Complete Halt to Acts of Sexual Violence against Civilians in Conflict Zones, unanimously adopting Resolution 1820 (2008)," SC/9364, United Nations Department of Public Information (June 19, 2008). Available on the www.un.org website.

[36] Ines Alberdi, "UNIFEM Welcomes Security Council Resolutions 1888 and 1889," UNIFEM (October 5, 2009), http://www.unifem.org/news_events/story_detail.php?StoryID=943 (accessed March 8, 2010).

[37] Stop Rape Now, "Stop Rape Now: UN Action against Sexual Violence in Conflict." Available on the www.stoprapenow.org website.

[38] United Nations Security Council, "Resolution 1888 (2009)" (September 30, 2009).

[39] Secretary-General, United Nations, "Secretary-General Appoints Margot Wallström of Sweden as Special Representative on Sexual Violence in Conflict," United Nations, Department of Public Information (February 2, 2010). Available on the www.un.org website.

[40] Jennifer Simon, "UN Appoints Special Representative on Sexual Violence in Conflict," Council on Women and Girls, United States (February 10, 2010). Available on the www.whitehouse.gov website.

[41] Margot Wollström, quoted in Amy Lieberman, "UN Appoints Wallström Special Representative for Sexual Violence," *Europa Newswire* (February 9, 2010). Available on the www.europanewsblog.com website.

[42] Copelon, "Surfacing Gender," 73.

[43] Nira Yuval-Davis, "Gender, the Nationalist Imagination, War, and Peace," in Giles and Hyndman, *Sites of Violence*, 183.

[44] Cynthia Cockburn, "The Continuum of Violence: A Gender Perspective on War and Pace," in Giles and Hyndman, *Sites of Violence*, 39.

[45] Julie A. Mertus, *War's Offensive on Women: The Humanitarian Challenge in Bosnia, Kosovo, and Afghanistan* (Bloomfield, CT: Kumarian Press, 2000), 10.

[46] Ibid., 11–12.

[47] Jennifer Hyndman, "Refugee Camps as Conflict Zones: The Politics of Gender," in Giles and Hyndman, *Sites of Violence*, 193.

[48] Women's Refugee Commission, *Peril or Protection: The Link between Livelihoods and Gender-based Violence in Displacement Settings* (New York: Women's Refugee Commission, November 2009), 5.

[49] Human Rights Watch, "Uncertain Refuge: International Failures to Protect Refugees," *A Human Rights Watch Short Report* 9, no. 1 (April 1997): 16.

[50] Hyndman, "Refugee Camps as Conflict Zones," 194.

[51] Sheila Meintjes, Anu Pillay, and Meredith Tershen, "There Is No Aftermath for Women," in *The Aftermath: Women in Post-Conflict Transformation*, ed. Sheila Meintjes, Anu Pillay, and Meredith Tershen (London: Zed Books, 2001), 15.

[52] Ibid., 16.

[53] Heaven Crawley, "Engendering the State in Refugee Women's Claims for Asylum," in Jacobs, Jacobson, and Marchbank, *States of Conflict*, 92. On the politics of gender of asylum, see also Jane Freedman, "Women Seeking Asylum: The Politics of Gender in the Asylum Determination Process in France," *International Feminist Journal of Politics* 10, no. 2 (June 2008): 154–72.

[54] Crawley, "Engendering the State in Refugee Women's Claims for Asylum," 93–94.

[55] Ibid., 95.

[56] Freedman, "Women Seeking Asylum," 161. On the UNHCR Handbook for the Protection of Women and Girls (2008), see Mulki Al-Sharmani, "Navigating Refugee Life," *UN Chronicle*, available on the un.org website.

[57] Human Rights Watch, "Uncertain Refuge," 16.

[58] Ibid., 17.

[59] Ibid.

[60] Crawley, "Engendering the State in Refugee Women's Claims for Asylum," 101.

[61] UNHCR (written by Erin K. Baines), *Respect Our Rights: Partnership for Equality: Report on the Dialogue with Refugee Women, June 20–22, 2001* (December 2001), 9.

[62] Ibid., 10.

[63] Ibid., 11.

[64] Ibid., 20.

[65] As quoted in ibid., 32.

[66] Women's Refugee Commission, *Peril or Protection*, 1.

[67] Mary Caprioli and Kimberly Lynn Douglass, "Nation Building and Women: The Effect of Intervention on Women's Agency," *Foreign Policy Analysis* 4 (2008): 49.

Chapter 4

Women, Political Activism, and Conflict

Chapter 3 focused on the ways in which women are affected by social and political conflict and violence. In this chapter we address the ways in which women respond politically once a conflict occurs. Our focus here is on what women choose to do *during* the conflict in order to engage in some form of political action as they are faced with increasingly difficult and changing circumstances, including becoming heads of household, the additional burden of caring for survivors and children, accessing food, sexual violence and/or exploitation, and so forth.[1] In other words, our emphasis is on the choices that women feel are available to them during situations of conflict, and on understanding which ones they make and why. Our assumption is that they will make those choices that give them a sense of power and agency at a time when much in their lives seems out of their control.

We are looking at conflict as a continuous process in which what happens at each phase affects subsequent phases. What we are most interested in are the types of political action that women take during conflict that lead into and affect the roles they play during the process of peace negotiation/conflict resolution, and then post-conflict restructuring (which is explored in more detail in the next chapter). Specifically, we want to know how women's perceived roles at various stages affect their choice of actions.

What follows is a discussion of women's political activism focusing specifically on the periods in which the state exists in a situation of conflict. Our goal here is to identify the approaches that women have taken and to gauge the success of their actions. The chapter begins with a discussion of conflicts and their legacy of colonialism, which often provided the backdrop for the issues under contention among competing groups within the state. We move to a discussion of women's activism in conflict and war, how women establish networks, engage in the fighting as belligerents, or become "accidental activists." We then examine two broad types of conflict: societies in violent internal conflict, and societies in which there are social and political divisions but outright civil war is absent. In the section on the second broad type of internal conflict, we look at two case studies (South Africa and Cyprus) to understand the connection between societies with significant divisions and women's responses to those situations. We conclude with a brief overview of the main themes of the chapter.

Women and Conflict Zones

A range of responses is possible for women during conflict situations, from doing nothing to becoming engaged actively either in support of the conflict or to resolve the conflict, that is, by working for peace. Included in this possible range of behaviors or actions is the option to rely upon traditional roles (wife, mother, and daughter) generally located within the private sphere, or by opting for actions that are overtly feminist, often in defiance of traditional norms. Even in the most traditional societies women can make the conscious choice to move beyond the private sphere and into the public realm by becoming politically active and engaging with the formal political structure directly or indirectly. The latter form of activism might involve more than working within the political system. For example, in some cases women might choose to create organizations or movements that exist outside the formal political structure but that are designed to put pressure on it (as noted in Chapter 2). It is in this category of active engagement that some women have been successful by drawing on traditional roles around which women—and men—can coalesce. Often the roles that women either play or are placed into prior to or during a conflict will have a direct impact on the options available to them after the conflict ends. Because the direction that women's political activism will take after the war ends has its origins in the period of conflict, it is important to understand these as a whole.

Societies do not erupt into internal conflicts—ethnic, civil, and/or religious wars—without some prior warning or notice. Often the changes that take place within the society have the greatest impact on women who are most sensitive to those changes. Yet, women have the least amount of access to the political system and therefore the least opportunity to make or even influence the decisions that could avert conflict. Their options once conflict begins are limited: to stay and hope that they can survive the conflict, to leave and become a refugee, or to engage in some form of political action either in support of the conflict or working to end the conflict, which also can help set the stage for the post-conflict society.

We noted in Chapter 2 the changing notion of warfare since the end of the Cold War, and we used Goldstein as the reference point for the cases of "lethal intergroup violence" that will provide the guidelines for determining the examples we include in our analysis. For a number of reasons we are most interested in looking at those conflicts that are internal to a state.

Internal civil conflicts have proliferated since the end of the Cold War for a number of reasons. According to Krishna Kumar, all intrastate conflicts "share five broad characteristics relevant to women and gender studies." Some of these are more relevant to our work than others, but all are important. First, violence is intentionally committed against civilians by the warring parties. Second, large numbers of people are displaced by civil conflicts. Along with that, "often, the traditional roles of men and women are redefined, and the family institution comes under severe stress, resulting in divorce and desertion." The third characteristic is "women's own participation in civil wars [that] contributes to the redefinition of their identities and traditional roles." And she adds that, as is the case with men, women are victims of violence as well as perpetrators of violence in times of conflict.[2] Kumar's fourth characteristic is that in the course of a civil war, the belligerent parties deliberately engage in the destruction of "the supporting civilian infrastructure." And fifth, civil wars "leave a legacy of anger, bitterness, and hatred among the belligerent groups that is difficult to heal." This is especially true because, once the conflict ends, the parties to the conflict "continue to face each other daily" if the country has not been partitioned.[3]

In addition, civil conflicts are more likely to change the parameters of the battlefield, bringing the violence into the home in a number of different ways, not only through invasion by the opposition or the enemy, but through the growth of paramilitaries, an increase in domestic violence that often accompanies a militarized society, and, of course, through rape and sexual violence as tools of war, as noted in Chapter 3.

Intrastate, or civil, conflict pits one group against another within a single state. The growth of ethnic, religious, tribal, and national conflicts within a single state means that those who live together turn on one another; former friends can quickly become enemies; and even family members who are from different ethnic or religious groups can become adversaries.[4] Not only does this place women into positions where they must choose sides, but, we contend, it also affords them opportunities to become politically active, gaining power and agency as they work for conflict resolution and peace.

Because civil conflicts take place close to home, they also give women greater opportunity to make a difference, whether at the national or, more likely, the grassroots or community level. Although the fact that women have been active in working for causes pertaining to peace is not a new phenomenon, we contend that civil conflicts can accelerate this process, often drawing on women's traditional roles as wives and mothers as the basis for commonality that allows women to be active participants, at least in the short term, because, as various cases demonstrate, the patriarchal structure of society usually is not transformed once the conflict ends.

Cynthia Cockburn puts the relationship between men and women that now defines most social and political structures in broad historical perspective: "What is clear is that from around the beginning of the third millennium before the Christian era all societies have been patriarchal. That is to say, men have dominated women, in the family and by extension in all significant social institutions."[5] Cockburn continues that there were some sound reasons for the division in responsibility, but as she also notes, as Europe moved from a feudal system to capitalism, one of the shifts was from a "literal 'rule of the father' to more simply, 'the rule of men.'"[6] Gradually, governments, education systems, businesses, the military, religious orders, all ordered by men, effectively left women out of the decision-making/ power structures. Women's domain was the home and family, or the private sphere. This patriarchal structure is found in all states, including those of former European colonies. Consequently, in considering many, but not all, of these conflicts, it is important to remember that they have their origins in a colonial experience in which the colonial power sought to replicate the political, social, and economic structure of the imperial power in the colony. This, in turn, meant replicating a patriarchal structure that excluded women. Hence, while women were not decision-makers in the colonizing country, it was assumed or ensured that they would be excluded from decision-making or any position of power in the colony.

Over time, as the nature of warfare changed, so did the scope of the battlefield; the home was no longer a protected area. This meant that women's territory was no longer off limits and that women were thrust into the center of the conflict, whether they wanted to be or not. Furthermore, while women were concerned about their husbands and sons, who were the ones who fought the wars, increasingly women and girls became involved either as active participants (engaged in combat, peace activism) and/or as victims of the violence. What did not change was women's exclusion from the decision-making process that leads to conflict within a state.

While larger international conflicts have many of these same characteristics, we think that those wars, in some ways, are further removed from women and that the barriers to women's involvement are far greater in those cases (of course, we do not discount the role that transnational women's antiwar groups have played in seeking an end to conflicts). As Kumar's characteristics make clear, the fact that after a civil conflict ends, the belligerents are forced to live together, makes women's roles during conflict both more difficult but also more important. Women who can begin to work together *during* the conflict are in a stronger position to help knit the society together *after* the conflict ends.

In examining women's political activism during conflict, we are not looking only at actions that are self-identified as feminist in nature or by design. Rather, we want to understand what types of actions women choose to engage in and why. It is in understanding their motivation that it should become clear whether the women see their actions as feminist or not. For example, in more traditional societies the motherist position can be an acceptable springboard to political action that is couched in personal terms, such as the need to keep "our sons" from dying in war. This approach could allow women's activism to be accepted in a way that it might not be otherwise. Or, in some cases, the role of mother actually elevates women's positions, giving them additional credibility and even power. The concern, as Helen Callaway points out, is that emphasizing women's roles as mothers and wives in cases of internal political conflict "presents a contradiction: the value given to female roles emphasizes gender polarity, thus strengthening male roles as the dominant structure."[7]

Anderlini notes that some mothers groups, such as the Argentine Mothers of the Plaza de Mayo, are "typically pacifist and often feminist." And she notes that "by embracing and strategically using the motherhood identity . . . they are simultaneously reaching out widely to women and directly challenging the moral authority of states that typically define themselves through social conservatism heavily dosed with militarism and traditional family values that uphold motherhood as the ultimate virtue."[8] In such cases women choose to integrate what would be the traditional and private with the public and often feminist in order to take a political stand. In the case of the Bosnian War, antiwar women's groups (both refugee and non-refugee women) comprised women who, according to Maja Korac, "had not necessarily ever considered themselves to be feminist." Yet, through their work in these groups, which focused on women who experienced and survived the sexual violence committed against them during the war, they became increasingly aware of the "particularities of the position of women and gender dimensions of war and violence." Through that increased awareness, women formed "counter-narratives of belonging from their experience of war and exile," counter-narratives that could have played a role in the peace building process once the war ended.[9]

What will be demonstrated in this chapter and the next, however, is that in most societies, when the conflict ends, women's access to decision-making, including decisions and policies related to improving women's lives, does not increase. As Callaway astutely notes, women tend to put "others—their children, husbands and community—ahead of themselves. The political conflict enlisted their energies but inhibited collective action to promote women's interests."[10] The challenge is how to harness the new political identities and roles women have acquired in times of war for greater representation and an elevated place at the peace negotiations and post-conflict reconstruction process, and a change in the gender power structure of society.[11]

Zones of Conflict

In her study of women's political activism and resistance in Israel, Tami Jacoby writes that "zones of peace refer to North American and Western Europe, where relative peace and freedom from war is enjoyed along with high levels of prosperity and economic and political cooperation. By way of contrast to the development of women's movements in peaceful areas, non-Western women have tended to become politicized within the broader contexts of civil-ethnic conflicts and developing states." Jacoby argues that in those zones of conflict, "women mobilize alongside their men, whether to liberate the society from colonial or post-colonial oppression, to campaign for national self-determination, or to partake in the process of democratization."[12]

We think that the concept of zones of conflict actually is far broader than the geographic boundaries noted above. Thus, to broaden Jacoby's definition, a zone of conflict can be found wherever there are deep social and political divisions that result in outbreaks of violence. Using that broader definition, such zones of conflict can be found in the Western/developed world, as in Northern Ireland, as well as in the non-Western/developing world. Civil, ethnic, religious, and other forms of internal conflict increasingly are associated with the developing world. Nonetheless, we think that the critical variable for women's politicization is not *where* the conflict is found as much as the circumstances surrounding it and the issue of how widespread the conflict is. Specifically, women are motivated to take political action when a conflict touches them directly in some way. In those cases women's political activism is guided not only by the conflict, but by social, economic, and cultural factors that have undoubtedly divided the society as well. For example, in Northern Ireland women were directly affected by the onset of the Troubles that accelerated in the 1960s, and yet in most cases they were removed from the decision-making, on both the Catholic and Protestant sides, that perpetuated the violence. As early as the 1970s women in both communities "mobilized against paramilitary violence" and saw themselves "as having a unique insight into the needs of the community and a special role to play in promoting the interests of the community."[13] But in the 1980s, as political issues were being discussed and negotiated, women were largely removed from the process. In fact, "many of the feminist activists were displeased with the fact that they were kept outside the policy making process in which women were underrepresented, a fact that seemed unlikely to change."[14]

It is important to note that this does not mean that "women's issues" were omitted from consideration by the dominant political parties that also perpetuated the violence. For example, the Sinn Fein Manifesto on Women, believed to date from 1989, begins by stating: "Women face significant difficulties in their daily lives as a result of long years of discrimination and injustice against them. This repression is deep-rooted, not merely, nor even primarily, legislative. We must all work to explore the manner in which legislation is used to oppress women, and highlight the way in which our own attitudes add to this oppression."[15]

This manifesto highlights the dichotomy that affected women within Northern Ireland, clearly a society in conflict: one of the major parties that perpetuated violence

Margaret Ward, director of the Women's Resource and Development Agency in Northern Ireland, follows issues pertaining to women in Northern Ireland. She noted in a conversation that Sinn Fein, the political wing of the Irish Republican Army (IRA), was extremely liberal in its recognition of many of the issues pertaining to women, a point that was confirmed in the Sinn Fein Manifesto.* However, she went on to note that even though women often appeared prominently at the side of Gerry Adams, leader of Sinn Fein, this did not necessarily mean that they actually had input into the decision-making of the group, which was primarily men's work.

* Kaufman, conversation with Margaret Ward, Belfast, Northern Ireland, November 20, 2007.

noted the discrimination that exists against women while also advocating a legislative (that is, official government) response to the situation. Yet at the same time, there were few women who served as official representatives from Northern Ireland to the British Parliament, who would have had jurisdiction over laws governing Northern Ireland, and there were virtually no women in the political decision-making hierarchy of Sinn Fein.

Given these political realities, what options are available to women as a country moves toward and into conflict? Since women generally are removed from direct decision-making, one option is to find ways to work outside the system and to influence the outcome of decisions. Another option is to try to break into the system and become a decision-maker or gain a seat at the table. This, too, generally requires working with other like-minded individuals (primarily women) who can help provide the support needed to confront the existing patriarchal structure. It is the creation of those networks prior to or even during conflict that can lead us to the answer to the question of what happens to the women after the conflict ends.

In looking at women's political activism prior to the outbreak of conflict, during it, and then working to resolve or end it, it is important to remember that what we are really looking at is a *process* that is dynamic and that can be injected at various stages. Seeing, sensing, or understanding the buildup toward conflict, women often become politicized and mobilized either to avert the conflict or to prepare for it. It is that mobilization that continues or accelerates during the conflict itself, especially as women and their families are directly affected by the onset of violence. The women's political activism that takes place during the conflict may be a continuation of the work started prior to the conflict, or it may be of a different nature once the conflict begins.

Women's Activism in Conflict Situations

Once the decision to act is made, one of the critical decisions that women make is in determining the *type* of actions in which to engage. Often the decision that women make depends upon their circumstances, and their perceptions of themselves. For example, as Kumar notes in the "Overview" introducing the cases in her volume, women in situations of civil and internal conflict often suffer from physical insecurity, psychological trauma, sexual abuse, economic disruption, and social upheaval, to name but a few of the issues that women confront.[16] While the effects of any of these can be harmful enough to women, often they suffer from more than one. Despite this, all the cases in her study—Rwanda, Cambodia, Georgia, Bosnia and Herzegovina, Guatemala, and El Salvador—"saw an expansion of women's public roles and responsibilities during conflict. The challenges of surviving the absence of men and the opportunities created by conflict contributed to this expansion."[17] In fact, these cases illustrate the ways in which women joined together to meet the needs created by the conflict, filling a vacuum and empowering them at the same time.

Maud Eduards states her assumption that "all human beings, by nature, have agency, the capacity to initiate change, to commit oneself to a certain transformative course of action, independently of historical circumstances." From this starting point, it follows logically that all human beings will want "to use this capacity in one way or another, to be an agent rather than a passive being, a victim. Put simply, given the chance, people will try to influence the course of events as much as possible, rather than sit back and suffer changes."[18]

Women who choose to take action during conflict as a way of gaining agency have a number of options. Some women choose to work for peace as a way to gain some sense of control over a situation of conflict or war, a decision that they were not involved with, while others clearly opt to engage as belligerents.

Women as Belligerents

Many of the reasons that enable women to work together to build networks across the divides that led to conflict are similar to the reasons women give for deciding to engage in acts of violence as a response to a conflict situation. For example, a profile of women activists in Gaza, done by National Public Radio in January 2007, illustrates how thin is the line between women's activism in support of peace and taking action by engaging in violence: "In conservative, male-dominated, clan-based Gaza, Palestinian women have long been forced to keep their opinions and ideas confined inside household walls. But in an important shift, Gaza women are increasingly taking action and expressing their views more and more in public." In this story, one woman, Naila Ayesh, who is the director of the Women's Affairs Center, an NGO based in Gaza, was quoted as saying, "'These women now go out of their homes asking to be part of stopping this violence inside our society.'"[19] One of the points that this story made was that while some of the women now turn out for political rallies and other public acts of political activism, some have turned to acts of violence, including acts of suicide bombing, as a way to have an impact. The decision to engage in some sort of political action empowers women in a way otherwise impossible in this traditional society.

Women's support for a conflict might include hiding and transporting weapons, serving as a lookout and providing a warning if government forces are approaching, taking up arms, or becoming a suicide bomber.[20] We can draw a number of conclusions about women's decisions to become active combatants as a form of political action rather than working for peace. First, it is apparent that women must be personally involved and committed to "the cause" (usually liberation), feel that they have a stake in the outcome, and want to get involved directly. Nationalist sentiment seems to be a given and is the rationale stated by women who engage in political violence in the cases of the former Yugoslavia (seen in Bosnia, Serbia, and Croatia), Sri Lanka, and numerous other cases of societies in conflict, especially for extended periods of time.

However, according to Miranda Alison, "nationalist fervor" is a "meta-reason." She argues that there are other, more personal factors that prompt women to engage in this type of action. Alison interviewed fourteen Tamil Tiger (LTTE) female combatants in Sri Lanka. She found that "LTTE women, like LTTE men, are primarily motivated by 'nationalist fervor.'" In this case, among the reasons women gave regarding their choice to join was that they were committed to the ideas of "freedom for the Tamil nation, self-determination, land and rights for Tamils." Alison helps provide clues as to some of the other motivations that women have for being combatants. She draws on her interviews as well as research to identify a range of factors which include "communal perception of suffering, oppression and injustice," and personal experiences, such as anger over the deaths of loved ones, which lead women to take up arms.[21]

To understand women's motivations it is necessary to delve deeper into the personal reasons women choose to become combatants or belligerents. Their choice might be due to the fact that the woman and/or a loved one was harmed or violated by the enemy, in which case the woman might seek revenge. Or it might be because such women want to make their society a better place for their children and other women. It is important to note that these are all reasons that other women gave in assessing their decision to work for peace in a society in conflict. In some instances women feel that they can have a more direct impact on the outcome by resorting to acts of political violence rather than working for peace.

In addition, women must feel not only a commitment to the "cause," but also believe that they have few options regarding ways in which they can get involved. Whether because their approach to the formal political process is blocked, which it most often is for women, or they have little formal training or education that would give them more options, they choose violence rather than peace. This ties to another important finding: women resort to acts of violence as a source of empowerment, something that they often do not experience in traditional, patriarchal societies. Hence, in looking for ways to acquire a sense of political agency, they choose a means that allows them to make a difference and to do so in support of a cause. For example, Tsjeard Bouta, Georg Frerks, and Ian Bannon found that many women who joined paramilitaries and militaries in El Salvador and Sudan gained leadership positions and responsibility during those conflicts.[22]

One of the most striking things about what Alison and others have found when looking at women who choose to engage in violence during situations of conflict is that their motivation for doing so is no different than men's. However, what makes this type of response interesting to examine is that it flies in the face of gender stereotypes of women as peaceful. As feminist scholars have repeatedly shown, understandings of masculinity and femininity are socially constructed, linked to women's and men's perceived "appropriate" behavior. This gendered perspective reinforces the essentialist nature of women as nurturers, caretakers, and peacemakers. Thus, when a woman engages in political violence rather than in actions to promote peace, the assumption is that she has somehow transgressed her gender identity and her role as peacemaker.[23] And yet, taking action, even violent action, is a way for women to gain agency in conflict.

While resorting to violence is one type of political action, we are interested in understanding women's decisions to work for peace during situations of conflict. While this might fit within the more traditional stereotypes of women's political activism, many scholars argue that women's approaches to peace offer a different perspective that may lead to a more durable and long-lasting peace. Swanee Hunt and Cristina Posa argue that the research "supports the stereotype of women as generally more collaborative than men and thus more inclined toward consensus and compromise." The fact that women are "second-class citizens" in most (all) societies "is a source of empowerment, since it has made women adept at finding innovative ways to cope with problems."[24] Women start building the networks necessary to work for peace during conflict, as women are drawn together by common needs, fears, and goals. It is this mobilization that takes place during the conflict that sets the stage for what happens during the period of conflict resolution and the process of negotiating for peace in terms of improving women's conditions and status in society after the conflict ends.

Women's Networking During Conflict

Examples abound of organizations founded by women at the grassroots level during periods of conflict in order to influence the government or other members of the society, or even to draw attention to the situation for those outside the country to influence them to intervene and help. These organizations are not necessarily so much about ending the conflict as about making the situation known to a broad audience. For example, Women in Black was started in Israel in 1988, according to its webiste, "by women protesting against Israel's Occupation of the West Bank and Gaza. Women in Black has developed in the United States, England, Italy, Spain, Azerbaijan and in FR [former] Yugoslavia, where women in Belgrade have stood in weekly vigils since 1991 to protest war and the Serbian regime's policies of nationalist aggression." Women in Black, like many women's groups, addresses more than simply issues of war and conflict; according to its website, it has broadened its mission to protest "rape as a tool of war, ethnic cleansing and human rights abuses all over the world." Because it was so inclusive in its approach, Women in Black was also successful at bridging the gap between Israeli and Palestinian women, allowing women on both sides to join together in pursuit of the common goal of peace, which provided an opportunity for the women to join not only in protest, but also in friendship.[25]

An explicitly feminist group transcended the ethnic divisions in the war in Bosnia. Established in 1993, the Medica Women's Therapy Center provided services to women who had experienced domestic violence. Women from various backgrounds (varying educational levels, rural and urban women) staff the center. According to Cynthia Cockburn, women shared the view that, regardless of their ethnic identity, they had a commonality of experience (sexual violence, domestic violence) as women. This "commonality" became the unifying element for these women to come together in spite of the ethnic divisions of their society.[26]

In the case of Northern Ireland, women's groups linking Protestant and Catholic women emerged from the community level in the midst of the violence of the Troubles. Bernadette (Devlin) McAliskey, who rose to prominence in the late 1960s as an activist leader on the Catholic/Republican side, now talks about the "small histories" that created a women's network, allowing them to be physically safe from violence (domestic and political) during the height of the Troubles in Northern Ireland. But in creating these networks, they were also building an infrastructure that would help lead to peace. In her view that infrastructure was being built every day in the rural areas during the conflict. And she attributes this to a "feminine way of working" that involves recognizing the importance of working together.[27] The goal here was not necessarily working for peace as much as bridging the gaps that contributed to the onset of the conflict initially by finding common ground.

In Liberia in the 1990s, when the advent of warlords "was devastating the nation and a dozen peace agreements [were] in shreds," a schoolteacher and her friends "decided to mobilize women 'to bring pressure on the warlords to stop the fighting.'" Eventually, over four hundred women showed up for a mass meeting and "the Liberians demonstrated and built public support and legitimacy. The Liberian Women's Initiative (LWI) was born." In 1996, the warring parties "agreed to end fighting and hold elections." Anderlini notes that the LWI played a vital role in that process.[28] And there are other examples—Colombia, Sri Lanka, and South Africa,

Bernadette Devlin McAliskey rose to prominence in the 1960s as one of the leaders of the then-nascent civil rights movement in Northern Ireland. The primary issues that were raised by the Catholic protestors were about the discrimination against them in a range of issues, including access to housing and jobs, and to protest what was called "British indifference to the need for reform in Northern Ireland."* Despite—or because of—the fact that she was a woman, Bernadette Devlin emerged as one of the major leaders of the marches. Elected to Parliament in 1969, when she was twenty-one years old, the youngest woman elected, she served as a Member of Parliament until 1974. Now retired, since 1997 she has served as coordinator of the South Tyrone Empowerment Programme and continues to work for human rights causes in Northern Ireland.**

* Tim Pat Coogan, *The Troubles: Ireland's Ordeal and the Search for Peace* (New York: Palgrave, 2002), 69.
** For more information about Devlin and her rise as a political activist, see Bernadette Devlin, *The Price of My Soul* (New York: Vintage Books, 1969).

to name a few—of women joining together at the grassroots or community level during conflict, bonded by common concerns.

These cases help support the contention that situations of conflict create needs that women have filled by working together, creating networks that could ultimately lead to political action, including resolution of the conflict, even if that was not the original intent. It is important to note that in the examples given above, the women's goals were not necessarily political, nor did many of these women think of themselves as political. Rather, as they came together to address a need that became more apparent during the conflict, they were united by shared experience. Their common goals not only motivated and mobilized them, but allowed them to work together despite the differences that might otherwise divide their society. One result was political action as the group became both more powerful and more empowered.

Here we can return to ideas put forward by Elisabeth Porter, who describes women as having the ability to "dialogue across differences." Porter describes this idea in more detail as follows:

Women constantly share each other's life stories and the myriad of details that make up mundane, ordinary lives, shared over the telephone, when walking children to school, over coffee when borrowing a household item or clothes. Talking through our narratives with those who come from different traditions, communities and regions is crucial to break the barriers of distrust that too often are based on fear cultivated through ignorance.[29]

Hence, despite the differences that might divide the society, women are united and mobilized into action by their common desires and dreams, including those for a better society after the conflict ends.

Anderlini points out that women peace activists "know and cope with the consequences of basic insecurity—the lack of education, health care, and sanitation and the fear of violence—but they also draw on their own strength and position in society to bring security for themselves and their dependents." In other words, these women come together and are held together by common experience that, in turn, breeds a sense of trust. But Anderlini makes another important point when she says "women activists focus their own efforts on changing entrenched attitudes and practices by finding their own entry points and building on their social ties."[30] Thus, there is no "one size fits all" approach. Instead, women learn to work within the constraints of their particular society, given their particular goals.

Especially during situations of conflict, women become mobilized to engage in political action when the situation affects them directly, when they can build ties with other women who have had similar experiences and who have similar goals, and when they can bring pressure to bear on the existing political structure in ways that are most familiar and comfortable to them. For women engaging in political activism during a period of conflict, this combination seems to be a recipe, if not for success (that is, conflict resolution and peace), at least for allowing their voices to be heard. It is also an important survival strategy to help them through a very difficult time.

Accidental Activists

In some cases women are thrust into political roles because of circumstances. In effect, it is up to women to determine how they want to respond to those circumstances of conflict and political violence and the appropriate political action to take. Monica McWilliams gives some examples in the case of Northern Ireland: "As it happened during the War of Independence in 1916, when women *were thrust* into political roles following the execution of the male leaders who had taken part in the Easter Rising, so it was in August 1971 when the women civil rights activists assumed the organizational roles of the men who had been arrested, following the introduction of internment." She refers to cases such as this as "accidental activism," a term coined by Susan Hyatt. McWilliams describes "accidental activism" as "the activism 'born of the immediate experience of social injustice, rather than as a consequence of a pre-existing ideological belief.'" According to this notion, "women who previously did not see themselves as in any way political became advocates and agents for social change."[31] Ruth Lister draws on this same concept to talk about "the transformative impact on women of engagement in informal politics," and then uses Hyatt's example of how a group of women on a housing estate (housing project) in England "were transformed into confident national campaigners as a result of a campaign, started around a kitchen table, against the installation of water meters in their homes."[32]

The point here is that engaging in political action brought about by responding to conflict can transform women so that even those who did not previously see themselves as political and/or feminist, but who find themselves fighting for a cause, discover how rewarding and important their contributions can be. Furthermore, where women are alienated or excluded from the formal political system, they become empowered by their activism. "Involvement in informal community based politics can help to generate the confidence and sense of self-esteem . . . need[ed] to be an effective political citizen."[33]

The fact that women may be accidental activists or become engaged in local or community-based issues without an explicitly feminist orientation does not in any way minimize or diminish the contribution that they make. Furthermore, this type of experience helps prepare women for engaging with the larger political system if and/or when that becomes necessary, a point that is be explored in more detail later.

Types of Conflict

It can be argued that virtually every political and social system is divided and in conflict, at the very least, between the "haves" and the "have nots." If one subscribes to the realist school, all relationships and interactions are inherently political in their struggle for power. Where this varies among states is when and whether those struggles become so great that they result in armed violence and civil war. In the case of Cyprus, for example, we see a country that is physically divided but where the divisions have become the norm. Despite the bi-communal work that a small group of activists (primarily women) have engaged in, for the rest of the country the stakes were not perceived as high enough to change the status quo when they were given the chance. South Africa represents a different case. Here the power balance shifted so that those who had been oppressed (blacks and "coloreds") became the group in power, although it can be argued that the coloreds or those of

"Catherine" serves as one example of an accidental activist in Northern Ireland. She is a Protestant woman who has been a community activist for eighteen years. She now works actively with the group Women Into Politics, encouraging other women to get involved from the grassroots level. When asked how she got involved, she tells the story of a bomb planted in her community, allegedly by the IRA, but at the wrong address. Rather than killing the Protestants it was intended for, it killed one of the few Catholics living in her community. That event, and the way that the community came together afterward, prompted her to begin working in her community for the betterment of all.[*]

[*] Kaufman conversation with "Catherine" in Belfast, May 29, 2006.

mixed race have not yet achieved full equality. In South Africa women were engaged in many aspects of the struggle, from those who worked in traditional roles as
wives and mothers at a grassroots community level, to those who were overtly feminist, to those who joined with men in fighting for their cause. However, in none of
these cases was women's work considered to be equal to men's.

Social and political conflicts can take many forms, all of which affect women
and have prompted political responses from them. These conflicts may or may not
be overtly violent, although a sense of insecurity, threat, and the fear of violence
certainly is always present in any divided society. What characterizes all these conflicts is the divisions within the society in which one group seeks to oppress or
dominate another for political advantage. The divisions might be ethnic, racial, or
religious, although in most cases those are excuses for what is, in reality, a struggle
for political power. And since the struggle is virtually always about political power,
it is framed by men. Here Haleh Afshar makes an important point about the impact of conflict on women. Regardless of the role that they play, women's participation is never seen as equal to or as important as the work done by men. This pattern, which starts during a conflict, is perpetuated after the conflict ends. Afshar
writes:

> In times of war, gender barriers were diluted. Where they were active com-
> batants, women's participation often helped during the time of war to create
> a sense of equality and erase gender differences. Sometimes individual wom-
> en have even been propelled into positions of authority. But those were the
> exceptions. All too often in the post-war era women have found it harder to
> maintain their positions. This may be because their participation was always
> seen as marginal; they were 'helpers' and not policy makers or frontline com-
> batants.[34]

Thus, women's roles, while important, were seen as subordinate to the roles played
by men. This not only has implications for what they do during conflict, but for the
roles that they play after the conflict ends. It also helps explain why, in general,
women often are not included in positions of political leadership subsequent to a
conflict.

In order to understand more about women's political activism during times of
conflict, we look at two broad categories: societies that are in violent and deadly
conflict, and those in which a conflict or social/political division is present, but
where violence is sporadic rather than ongoing. We explore women's political activism in the cause of conflict resolution or reaching across the political divides in
both cases to see whether there are differences in women's responses, depending on
whether the violence is overt or where the conflict is more covert.

Societies in Violent Conflict

Those instances where states are engaged in violent and deadly conflict represent circumstances in which women are forced to make significant choices, often with very high stakes. Those women who stay in a nation that is in the midst of violent conflict, either because of a conscious choice or of necessity, live in a militarized world in which the zone of conflict literally has invaded their homes. As Afshar notes, in those circumstances "violence becomes a crisis of everyday life, especially when 'dirty war' strategies are used by different factions contending for power. It becomes especially difficult, if not impossible, to separate combat from non-combat, and the frontguard and rearguard are not clear-cut either. Most women in such situations experience violence as a matter of daily life and devise strategies to cope with it."[35] They are often forced to get involved, either to work for one side or the other, or to work for peace by reaching out across the divides that split the country. Taking any position poses risks, but for many women, not taking a position is not an option.

In addition to making a political decision as to which side to support, women also frame their political action either as a feminist response to the situation or a more traditional response as a wife, mother, and woman. We cannot—nor should we—assume that all women's responses to and actions about being in a state of conflict will be the same. As Cockburn notes, "Armed conflict takes many forms." As such, it will generate "a diversity of responses."[36] Even those women who chose to work for peace had a range of ways of doing so. It is in understanding the options available and the particular choices the women made and why that we can increase our understanding of women and war and, ultimately, of what happened to those women.

For example, in their study of women in El Salvador during the civil war from 1980 through 1992, Martha Thompson and Deborah Eade describe the ways in which the conflict significantly altered the role of women in that country. Prior to the outbreak of the war, the culture was "intensely patriarchal and *machismo* reigned in the household. Women were under the control of their husbands; they had little access to education, and the concept of women's rights was unknown." They also note that gender roles were fixed; "Motherhood was women's major claim to dignity and respect, but that dignity was sentimentalized and devoid of economic rights or any legal claim."[37] But it was that same traditional perspective that actually allowed women to play a major role during the conflict, often using the gender stereotyping that had been so much a part of the society. Inger Skjelsbaek claims that the conflict provided opportunities for women to learn new skills as well as taking on "new responsibilities normally reserved for men," including combat roles.[38]

Thompson and Eade offer a number of examples of the ways in which women drew on the image of mother with child "to protect themselves and their communities."

In addition to the image of motherhood, their role as mother drew the women together, allowing them to form mutual support groups "where they could share their stories, take comfort from each other, and reflect on what had happened to them in terms of justice and rights." Even the young and single women "drew a great deal of strength from each other and their similar status as single childless women who nonetheless had a strong community."[39] The strength that these women derived from being part of a group of women with common interests helped them survive the conflict, but it also gave them the ability to play a role politically and even engage in combat.[40]

Anderlini notes that after the war, many of these women in El Salvador who had been so instrumental at organizing at the grassroots level—some had even served as combatants—faced various stigmas because of the ways in which they had flouted the taboos and then stepped back into traditional roles. However, many women also acknowledged in retrospect that it was their willingness to do so that helped the men reintegrate after the war, thereby fostering the postwar recovery process.[41] But in so doing, they undermined the strides they had made during the conflict, thereby returning women to the traditional and subservient roles that they had had prior to the conflict. According to Anderlini, at that point women had few choices. "Many wanted to return to normalcy and lives they had put on hold, but they also wanted to participate in community and public life. Yet the opportunities were few and far between, at times simply because child-care provisions were not available."[42]

In contrast to the case of El Salvador, in women's testimonies regarding the conflict in Uganda, Judy El-Bushra found that because women had accepted greater responsibilities during the conflict, they found these *harder* to give up after the conflict ended. On the other hand, men found it increasingly difficult to reintegrate back into the society after the war ended, especially with women reluctant to give up the "power" they had gained as a result of war. One of the reasons that the women were able to exert their independence was because of the organizations in which they were linked together. Local organizations of women led to women's increasing involvement "in peace-building initiatives and in support for, for example, raped and disabled women who are often also repudiated and without support."[43]

The case of Cambodia, a country torn by brutal civil war for almost thirty years, offers another perspective on the changing roles of women during conflict. In this case Kumar, Baldwin, and Benjamin note that "women's involvement in the political arena increased during the conflict" and that "the Khmer Rouge were the first to organize women at the grass-roots level." They established a "women's wing of the Communist Party," and the communist government that succeeded the Khmer Rouge "took major steps to enhance women's participation in the political process." While some scholars argue that "the regime did so because men were reluctant to serve in these groups," in fact, like many other communist regimes, "the government was committed to promoting gender equality."[44] Of course, the irony is that the Khmer Rouge was also committed to a brutal campaign of ethnic cleansing that left anywhere from between 1 and 3 million dead. It also led to significant disruptions in family life and a concomitant decline in the traditional status given to women.

Since the cease-fire of 1991, after an initial decline in the participation of women in the political process, "communities are acknowledging that women entering local and national politics bring a different approach and perspective." According to one local politician, quoted by Anderlini, they want more women candidates "because women don't solve problems by force and gunpoint."[45] But their experiences under the Khmer Rouge and the communist government that followed drove many women from participating, resulting in a decrease in the number of women who were actively involved in the political process. According to Kumar, Baldwin, and Benjamin, this decline is the result of "war fatigue, political disenchantment, the unstable economic situation, and the assertion of the Khmer identity with its emphasis on women's traditional roles."[46] This started to change again with the 1998 elections, with more women subsequently becoming actively involved in the formal political process.

These examples tell us a number of things about the behavior of both men and women during conflict that affect their role after the conflict ends. First, conflict prompts women to take on new roles within their society. Even in the most traditional societies the absence of men requires that women engage in actions that they were barred from prior to the conflict. Whether it was in the home, working for peace, or working in leadership positions in their community and/or in the government, conflict prompted women to advance in some ways. However, what is more telling is how few of those advances continued after the conflict. Either because women no longer wanted those roles or men returning from war did not want women to have them, in most cases women reverted to their pre-conflict roles and positions after the conflict ended.

In the cases where women did remain actively involved after the conflict ended, it was the networks they had built and connections they had made during the conflict that allowed them to continue. The roles that they took on during conflict, either by necessity or by choice, empowered them and gave them credibility that they might not have had without the conflict. These feelings continued after the end of conflict. This further supports the contention that violent conflict can change—and sometimes advance—women's gender roles, although not necessarily the gender power structures.[47] To some extent what happens after the conflict will be the result of a change in perceptions, both of the women and of the society, regarding women's roles and responsibilities and what might be considered the norm. (We explore this further in Chapter 6.)

Social and Political Divisions, Absent Violent Civil War

A country need not be engaged in a bloody and violent civil war to exist in a state of conflict. Johan Galtung notes that "the absence of war does not mean peace."[48] In fact, Galtung makes it clear that whenever a person, a group, or a nation-state "is displaying the means of physical violence, whether throwing stones around or testing nuclear arms, there may not be violence in the sense that anyone is hit or hurt, but there is nevertheless the *threat of physical violence* and indirect threat of mental violence that may even be characterized as some type of psychological violence since it constrains human action" (emphasis in original).[49] Hence, a country or society may exist in a state of conflict including a sense of threat, competition between or among different groups, and the threat that violence could erupt at any time without the presence of overt acts of violence. The critical point is an absence of a sense of physical security and safety.

The Troubles that afflicted Northern Ireland is an example of a conflict situation that had its root in a struggle for economic and political power as well as religious divisions, and where women's political activism can be found at all levels. Cyprus is an example of a country that has been divided for decades and that has experienced relatively few outbreaks of violence in the recent past. In fact, in that case, division seems to have become the status quo. South Africa is a country where women played a critical role in the fight against apartheid.

In the period since the end of the Cold War there have been many examples of violent conflict (many of which began during the Cold War). But looking at some of the instances in which there is a divided society characterized by the *threat* of violence by one group against another, rather than existing in a situation of ongoing violent conflict, can also be instructive. This does not suggest that there were not instances of armed violence; there were. But these cases, primarily Cyprus and South Africa, can be seen more as divided societies with ever-present tensions rather than ones engaged in outright civil war. In both cases the role that women played is instructive. In Cyprus a small group of women took the lead in bi-communal activities, although these have come to naught thus far. In South Africa, in contrast, women were actively involved in all aspects of the struggle against apartheid and for equality for all.

South Africa: A Case Study

Even though it was not overtly violent, the apartheid regime of South Africa is one type of political and social conflict that propelled women into political and even military action. It is also a case where "militarized nationalism" became the norm, and where "women are effectively the shock absorbers of the social dislocations which are the legacy of many years of war in the region."[50] In fact, as Jacklyn Cock notes, the legacy of the conflict in southern Africa "includes a militarized national-ism that regards violence as a legitimate way of dealing with conflict and means of obtaining and defending power. In addition, there are deep inequalities in access to resources, social tensions and a prevalence of antagonistic social identities often defined in ethnic and racial terms."[51] For that country, the process of conflict reso-lution and the peace building that followed not only engaged women deeply but is an example of how women's role in the process helped ensure that the country could move beyond its past to create a democratic state with putative equality.

Some of the issues that beset South Africa and had long-term implications for the country stemmed from its colonial history. Initially, the conflict was between the British and the Dutch (Boers), but in the process, it was the people of South Africa, especially the women, who suffered. The conflict between the Boers and the British resulted in British victory; in 1910 the Union of South Africa was created as a self-governing dominion of the British Empire. In 1912 the South African Native National Congress was founded, which later became the African National Congress (ANC). Despite its goal of eliminating restrictions against blacks and people of color, the constitution ensured that power stayed in the hands of whites, who con-tinued to pass laws restricting the rights and freedoms of non-whites. All-white elections held in 1948 brought to power the National Party, which put into place a strict policy of white domination and racial separation that became known as apart-heid. Through the 1970s and 1980s the international community became more assertive at enacting policies to pressure the South African government to eliminate this policy. Various embargoes were imposed on the country in the hope that the economic pressure would be sufficient. However, the sanctions were not effectively enforced and the policy continued.

Popular uprisings by blacks in some of the townships were more effective at bringing pressure on members of the government. Through the 1980s the level of violence increased as the police "were given immense powers and immunity through laws that protected them from being prosecuted for the human rights abuses they committed." At the same time, the "liberation army of the ANC stepped up its struggle against apartheid and engineered several bombings of strategic targets. This intensified the violence between the government and the ANC."[52]

In 1986, in the midst of this increasing violence, secret discussions started be-tween members of the government and Nelson Mandela, who had been impris-oned in the early 1960s on charges of treason. In February 1990, then-president F. W. de Klerk started to reverse some of the policies of the apartheid regime. Shortly thereafter, Mandela was released from prison. The country held its first nonracial elections in April 1994, and Nelson Mandela was installed as the country's first black president in May 1994. Given the history of the country, where were the women?

It is against the framework of the struggle for equality and against apartheid that the role of women in South Africa must be assessed. Shireen Hassim makes the point that "the extent to which women's movement activists in South Africa were able to harness and develop feminist consciousness was determined by the extent to which nationalist movements and other social movements were willing to allow feminist approaches to thrive." She also reminds us that "women do not mobilize as women simply because they are women. They may frame their actions in terms of a range of identities, whether as worker, student, African, white, and so on. In other words, women do not mobilize for a single reason."[53] In their struggle for power and against apartheid, Afshar makes the point that "some ANC and South African guerrilla women chose to be both lovers and fighters." However, it also placed the burden on them to prove that their choice had not "weakened" them or softened their position, as these two roles were often seen as mutually exclusive.[54]

Women's roles in South Africa in the fight against apartheid, as well as the reconciliation and rebuilding process that followed, were many and varied. Afshar notes that women served as freedom fighters, "where they were trained and fought along with men in the ANC forces. The ANC offered the same military training for men and women."[55] But, as Cock notes, even though women were actively involved with the ANC and the fight against apartheid, there was also "an absence of women from the leadership of the ANC and most organizations within the mass democratic movement." For black women, especially, this created a situation of "triple oppression," since they "are located at the intersection of the three lines along which privilege runs—gender, race, and class."[56]

This is not to suggest that white women were privileged in South Africa; they were not. Cock notes: "There is only a small number of white women who have formal power and influence." What this also means is that women in South Africa, white and black, had to confront a society of inequality in which "there is an image of the tough but submissive female."[57] While white women were more advantaged than black women in terms of access to education, for example, women in general were subordinated to men. Clearly, this affected the ways in which women, black and white, mobilized for political action during conflict and the role that they played after apartheid.

As noted above, some women of color chose to participate as freedom fighters with the ANC. Others chose to fight against and resist apartheid in other ways. As in Northern Ireland, many of the women who were most actively engaged in this struggle were working-class women who did not see themselves as feminist. In fact, according to interviews that Cock conducted, the women explicitly rejected the idea of feminism, which they saw as "exclusively about the promotion of middle-class women's interests," something that was far from what these black political activists were fighting for. Unlike other cases, where women bonded in their common roles as wives and mothers, Cock found that in the case of South Africa "black women had very little support from white women. Historically, the appeal to motherhood has not proved to be a powerful and unifying case."[58] Thus, the splintered and bifurcated nature of the society was strong enough to divide women in this case, rather than unite them on the areas in which they ostensibly shared common ground. An exception to this was the organization Black Sash, which was started by white women with a mandate to reach out to and work with black women.

In South Africa black women had to choose the type of political action that would work for them given the range of constraints and barriers imposed upon them. Furthermore, their actions can be seen as existing within two phases: the struggle to end apartheid, and the peacebuilding and reconciliation that followed.

Consistent with other cases, many women associated with the ANC defined their activism in terms of assuring their basic needs. As Hassim notes, "The everyday organization of women around their roles as mothers and community members by far outweighs the number of women engaged in overt political activities." But she also states that "a deeper analysis of women's political organizations suggests that the strategic links and cultural affinities between those organizations and the 'apolitical' women's groups are more extensive than is generally credited."[59]

This relationship, while overt, is something that is common across a range of women's organizations in a number of different countries and represents an important finding. Specifically, although women consider themselves to be "apolitical" and see their organizations as working to meet women's basic needs, in effect, the very nature of the organizations and what they are trying to do is inherently political, whether the women realize or acknowledge that or not. Cock even gives an example of a woman guerrilla fighter who noted: "I'm a guerrilla *because* I am a mother. . . . We have a better South Africa for our children. I do it for the children—all the children" (emphasis in original). This same woman, when asked about her experiences, stated that she has "a strong commitment to equal rights for women, but does not consider herself a feminist. She equates feminism with bra-burning and a denial of femininity."[60]

In South Africa women's political activism was bound up in the causes of nationalism and against apartheid often at the expense of working for women's rights. Hence, although women were actively engaged in the fight against apartheid, these activists "had little consensus about the necessity of or the most appropriate organizational forms for gender-based activism."[61] However, as Anderlini notes, "the South African women who fought for liberation from apartheid in the ANC recognized that to attain equality and self-determination they had to address the gender dynamics in their own political structures."[62]

This suggests that the oppression of apartheid combined with the gender-based discrimination of the society mobilized women to take political action. However, the type of action, the organizations that they engaged with, and even their goals were many and varied. And, as we have also seen in other cases, much of women's political activism was community based, because that was the area women knew best—given that they did not have access to the national decision-making level—and in which they could have an impact.

Cyprus: Another Case Study

The island of Cyprus represents an interesting case of a divided society where women's political activism became an important facet of cross-communal cooperation and reconciliation, although it did not lead to a successful conclusion of the issue. The Turkish military invasion of Cyprus in 1974 ultimately led to the division of the island, although, as Sumantra Bose notes, "the island is no stranger to turbulence. Virtually its entire history as a country since it gained independence from Britain in 1960 is a saga of turmoil and violence."[63] However, what we are most interested in is not the early period of the division but the later period, when women's groups led the way for cross-communal activity.

The difficulty of communication between the two sides of the island meant that cross-communal communication, when it took place, was facilitated by third parties, primarily organizations or groups from the United States. When there *was* face-to-face contact, it often took place out of the country. What is especially relevant here, as Cynthia Cockburn reports in her study of women in Cyprus, is that women "have been particularly active in this [reconciliation] process and may even have been a majority of bi-communalists." However, she also notes that those men or women "actively seeking contact with their counterparts [on] the other side of the Line have been a small minority of either population." Cockburn also illustrates clearly how difficult it is to move beyond the divisions in a society in conflict when she writes that "a whole generation of young people have grown up without first-hand knowledge of those who live on the other side, and their schooling has continued to convey a sense of 'them' as a source of enmity and danger."[64]

In general, women, who were largely left out of the leadership positions of the political parties, trade unions, and so on, were also the ones who were drawn to many of the cross-communal programs. Often these programs were facilitated by women who came from outside the island; the women from Cyprus were willing to be trained in conflict resolution and negotiation techniques, and then apply that training in pursuit of their goal of reaching across the communities. Furthermore, as accession to the European Union became a possibility, many of these women also grasped the importance of taking advantage of the circumstances to work together in pursuit of bi-communal communication.

In the case of Cyprus, then, while women were largely excluded from the political decisions that divided the island and kept it divided, they played a significant role in engaging in bi-communal activities. These were primarily informal and existed outside the bounds of the formal political structure and processes.

There are a number of lessons to be learned from the case of Cyprus, many of them negative, regarding the impact that women can—or cannot—have. Although women were actively engaged in bi-communal communication, these women represented only a small fraction of the population. The overall social and political structure is patriarchal; women have little access to decision-making, existing instead as "women's organizations" of the larger groups, such as political parties or trade unions, that set the priorities. The division of the island and the duration of that division have become entrenched. As noted above, there are generations who know nothing else. The education system as well as the myths and narratives have perpetuated the stories of the evils perpetrated by each side on the other. Taken together with the economic disparities that now exist between the prosperous south and the far poorer north, the divisions have become too entrenched to be overcome by a political "plan." While some women worked and continue to work for reconciliation, their efforts have not been enough to overcome the larger structural issues that keep the island divided and in a virtual state of conflict, albeit without violence.

Cyprus and South Africa are examples of countries that are or were in conflict without ongoing and sustained fighting. Nonetheless, they also illustrate the ways in which the division was sufficient to bring women together to create networks that, in turn, afforded them a measure of political power whether or not they were successful in achieving their desired goals. This suggests that any situation of conflict—any time a sense of security is undermined—creates the circumstances that encourage women to band together. This, in turn, empowers them to take action that they might not have been able to take otherwise.

Conclusion

This chapter looked at the ways in which conflict affected women. There was an increase in the insecurity of women; as countries became more militarized, so did the sanctity of the private realm, the home and family. This put women into the position of having to frame their responses to the situation but to do so within the context of a patriarchal framework within which their voices generally were not heard.

Clearly, women were able to use their traditional roles as an advantage during conflict by providing areas of commonality that allowed them to work together for a common cause. In many ways the grassroots activism that resulted defied the traditional roles that they were expected to play. The examples included here show that women were often thrust into a position of having to take some kind of action because of a conflict that significantly disrupted the social and political order. Hence, when the conflict resulted in an absence of men, who were fighting or killed, women stepped in to fill the void as political leaders and managers of the home. They often worked with other women to ensure a sense of security for themselves and their children, and they did so because they were forced to in the face of the insecurity that the conflict created. After the conflict ended, most women returned to their pre-conflict roles, either by choice or by the gender power structures that prevented them from taking a prominent role in the formal political sphere. However, in other cases they did not return to the pre-conflict roles. Empowered during the conflict to take action, many women did not want to give that up. What happened to those women after the conflict ended was a function of the men, as we saw in the cases of El Salvador and Uganda. In those cases where women retained the stronger role, what resulted was a restructuring of the society, most often at the local level, with at least an acknowledgment of the contributions that women can make.

However, the examples given also highlight another important point that can be seen in a number of cases: the relationship between the economic divide and the gender divide, which also prompts women to take political action. Any number of examples—South Africa, Cyprus, El Salvador, Northern Ireland, to name but a few—show the ways in which political and economic power is concentrated in the hands of the male elite (in the case of Northern Ireland, the Protestants), at the expense of other groups and women. For many women this resulted in awareness of the need to address the gender inequities that were embedded in the society if their country was ever to move to a situation of true equality after conflict. For example, South African women in the ANC who were engaged in the liberation struggle understood that changing the gender power structure within the organization was needed as part of the larger goal of self-determination and equality.[65] Thus, what might have started as political activism precipitated by conflict grew into awareness of and the need to fight for equality for women. One of the unintended consequences of women's political action during conflict was that the mobilization that started during the conflict helped provide a framework for them to work toward that larger goal.

One of the most consistent patterns we have found is that women started to coalesce and work for peace early in the process, often even as the society was beginning to move toward conflict. Certainly the groundwork was set during conflict for working toward peace. Specifically, women were creating the structures, organizations, and networks that would enable them to work together as a cohesive group to help facilitate the process of peace and reconciliation in the post-conflict society. Often, these were informal and necessary parts of ensuring the protection and security of women and children during the conflict. They also had the consequence—unintended or deliberate—of giving women a framework on which to build.

One of the more interesting findings is that in many cases the patriarchal structure of the country was the legacy of a colonial past, in which men were privileged and women were expected to play a more traditional role. But accompanying that was a parallel framework within which certain social/religious/ethnic groups were privileged at the expense of others. This social and political schism was a direct contributor to many of the conflicts that affected women in multiple ways. However, it should also be noted that in some societies it was the very essence of women's traditional roles as mothers, for example, that elevated them and gave them credibility and power, thereby enabling them to work against the dominant political structure.

Women often took the lead in working for peace through a grassroots effort, in part because that was the only option available to them. As it turns out, many of the male political leaders had a vested interest in seeing the divisions continue. In the case of Northern Ireland, for example, shortly after the Good Friday agreement was signed, one woman remarked that the people had wanted peace for a long time. It was the leaders of the various factions who benefited by keeping the conflict going.[66]

What we have learned here is that conflict has been extremely important in engaging women to take political action. Further, the impact of those actions far exceeded the immediate goals of addressing the conflict situation, including engaging women to work for peace and the betterment of their society after the conflict ends. Often, this was an unintended consequence of women's political activism during the conflict.

Notes

[1] Donna Pankhurst, "The 'Sex War' and Other Wars: Towards a Feminist Approach to Peace Building," *Development in Practice* 13, nos. 2/3 (May 2003): 159; Azza Karam, "Women in War and Peacebuilding," *International Feminist Journal of Politics* 3, no. 1 (April 2001): 3–6.

[2] Krishna Kumar, "Introduction," in *Women and Civil War: Impact, Organizations, and Action*, ed. Krishna Kumar (Boulder, CO: Lynne Rienner, 2001), 6–7.

[3] Kumar, "Introduction," 6–7.

[4] Women in ethnically or religiously "mixed marriages" was one of the variables that we examined in *Women, the State, and War*. Marriage is one way that states gender citizenship, and as we saw in the cases we examined, generally it is the woman who suffers when she marries outside her group. She is often ostracized by her own family and never really accepted by her husband's family. In some cases, as we saw in the case of former Yugoslavia, that has led directly to violence against women. See Joyce P. Kaufman and Kristen P. Williams, *Women, the State, and War* (Lanham, MD: Lexington Books, 2007), 96–103.

[5] Cynthia Cockburn, *From Where We Stand: War, Women's Activism and Feminist Analysis* (London: Zed Books, 2007), 240.

[6] Ibid.

[7] Helen Callaway, "Survival and Support: Women's Forms of Political Action," in *Caught Up in Conflict: Women's Responses to Political Strife*, ed. Rosemary Ridd and Helen Callaway (London: Macmillan, 1986), 228.

[8] Sanam Naraghi Anderlini, *Women Building Peace: What They Do, Why It Matters* (Boulder, CO: Lynne Rienner, 2007), 38–39.

[9] Maja Korac, "Gender, Conflict and Peace-Building: Lessons from the Conflict in the Former Yugoslavia," *Women's Studies International Forum* 29 (2006): 515.

[10] Callaway, "Survival and Support," 228.

[11] Virginia Sapiro, "Research Frontier Essay: When Are Interests Interesting? The Problem of Political Representation of Women," *American Political Science Review* 75, no. 3 (September 1981): 707.

[12] Tami Amanda Jacoby, *Women in Zones of Conflict: Power and Resistance in Israel* (Quebec: McGill-Queens University Press, 2005), 4.

[13] Carmel Roulston, "Women on the Margin: The Women's Movement in Northern Ireland, 1973–1995," in *Feminist Nationalism*, ed. Lois West (New York: Routledge, 1997), 45.

[14] Kaufman and Williams, *Women, the State, and War*, 163; see also Roulston, "Women on the Margin."

[15] Sinn Fein Manifesto on Women (1989), accessed at the Linen Hall Library, Belfast, Northern Ireland, November 2007.

[16] See Krishna Kumar, "Civil Wars, Women, and Gender Relations: An Overview," in *Women and Civil War: Impact, Organizations, and Action*, ed. Krishna Kuman, 5–26. Boulder, CO: Lynne Rienner, 2001.

[17] Ibid., 21.

[18] Maud L. Eduards, "Women's Agency and Collective Action," *Women's Studies International Forum* 17, nos. 2/3 (1994): 181.

[19] Eric Westervelt, "Middle East: Female Activists a Force in Male-Dominated Gaza," National Public Radio, *Morning Edition*, January 6, 2007. Available on the www.npr.org website.

[20] Callaway, "Survival and Support," 215; Miranda Alison, "Women as Agents of Political Violence: Gendering Security," *Security Dialog* 35, no. 4 (December 2004): 457.

[21] Miranda Alison, "Cogs in the Wheel? Women in the Liberation Tigers of Tamil Eelam," *Civil Wars* 6, no. 4 (Winter 2003): 40.

[22] Tsjeard Bouta, Georg Frerks, and Ian Bannon, *Gender, Conflict, and Development* (Washington DC: The World Bank, 2004), 54–55.

[23] Laura Sjoberg and Caron E. Gentry, *Mothers, Monsters, and Whores: Women's Violence in Global Politics* (London: Zed Books, 2007); J. Ann Tickner, *Gendering World Politics* (New York: Columbia University Press, 2001); J. Ann Tickner, *Gender in International Relations: Feminist Perspectives on Achieving Global Security* (New York: Columbia University Press, 1992).

[24] Swanee Hunt and Cristina Posa, "Women Waging Peace," *Foreign Policy* 124 (May–June 2001): 41.

[25] Elizabeth Warnock Fernea, *In Search of Islamic Fundamentalism* (New York: Anchor Books, 1998), 345–46; Kaufman and Williams, *Women, the State, and War*, 142.

[26] Cynthia Cockburn, *The Space between Us: Negotiating Gender and National Identities in Conflict* (London: Zed Books, 1998), 196–97.

[27] Bernadette Devlin McAliskey, "From Rural to Urban: A Rural View," talk given at Peace by Piece: Three Day International Women's Conference, Belfast, Northern Ireland, June 25, 2008.

[28] Anderlini, *Women Building Peace,* 56.

[29] Elisabeth Porter, "The Challenge of Dialogue Across Difference," in *Gender, Democracy and Inclusion in Northern Ireland,* ed. Carmel Roulston and Celia Davis (New York: Palgrave, 2001), 158.

[30] Anderlini, *Women Building Peace,* 12, 13.

[31] Monica McWilliams, "Struggling for Peace and Justice: Reflections on Women's Activism in Northern Ireland," *Journal of Women's History* 6/7, nos. 4/1 (Winter/Spring 1995): 19–20, 21.

[32] Ruth Lister, "Feminist Citizenship Theory: An Alternative Perspective on Understanding Women's Social and Political Lives," paper presented at Women and Social Capital, London South Bank University, April 2005.

[33] Lister, "Feminist Citizenship Theory," 23.

[34] Haleh Afshar, "Women and Wars: Some Trajectories towards a Feminist Peace," in *Development, Women, and War: Feminist Perspectives,* ed. Haleh Afshar and Deborah Eade (Oxford, UK: Oxfam Publishing, 2004), 45.

[35] Afshar, "Women and Wars," 47–48. When Joyce Kaufman was in Sarajevo in 2000, she interviewed a number of women who had remained in the city during the siege, which lasted from April 1992 until just after the signing of the Dayton Agreement in December 1995, making it the longest siege in modern history. When she asked the women how they were able to get through it, one of them simply said, "You just do."

[36] Cockburn, *From Where We Stand,* 13.

[37] Martha Thompson and Deborah Eade, "Women and War: Protection through Empowerment in El Salvador," in *Development, Women and War: Feminist Perspectives,* ed. Haleh Afshar and Deborah Eade (Oxford, UK: Oxfam, 2004), 224.

[38] Inger Skjelsbaek, "Is Femininity Inherently Peaceful? The Construction of Femininity in War," in *Gender, Peace and Conflict,* ed. Inger Skjelsbaek and Dan Smith (London: Sage, 2001), 58.

[39] Thompson and Eade, "Women and War," 233, 234.

[40] Skjelsbaek, "Is Femininity Inherently Peaceful?" 64.

[41] See Anderlini, *Women Building Peace,* 102–3.

[42] Anderlini, *Women Building Peace,* 118.

[43] Judy El-Bushra, "Transforming Conflict: Some Thoughts on a Gendered Understanding of Conflict Processes," in *States of Conflict: Gender, Violence, and Resistance,* ed. Susie Jacobs, Ruth Jacobson, and Jennifer Marchbank (London: Zed Books, 2000), 69–70.

[44] Krishna Kumar, Hannah Baldwin, and Judy Benjamin, "Profile: Cambodia," in *Women and Civil War: Impact, Organizations, and Action,* ed. Krishna Kumar (Boulder, CO: Lynne Rienner, 2001), 46. We found a similar pattern in the case of former Yugoslavia, where women advanced more professionally during the Tito regime than they did later. See Joyce

P. Kaufman and Kristen P. Williams, "Who Belongs? Women, Marriage, and Citizenship," *International Feminist Journal of Politics* 6, no. 3 (September 2004): 416–35.

[45] Anderlini, *Women Building Peace*, 127.

[46] Kumar, Baldwin and Benjamin, "Profile: Cambodia," 46–47.

[47] Pankhurst, "The 'Sex War' and Other Wars," 160–61; Sophie Richter-Devore, "Gender, Culture, and Conflict Resolution in Palestine," *Journal of Middle East Women's Studies* 4, no. 2 (Spring 2008): 39–40.

[48] Johan Galtung, cited in Ruth Jacobson, Susie Jacobs, and Jen Marchbank, "Introduction: States of Conflict," in Jacobs, Jacobson, and Marchbank, *States of Conflict*, 1.

[49] Johan Galtung, "Violence, Peace, and Peace Research," *Journal of Peace Research* 6, no. 3 (1969): 170.

[50] Jacklyn Cock, "Closing the Circle: Towards a Gendered Understanding of War and Peace" (July 2001). Available on the wb.uct.ac.za website.

[51] Ibid.

[52] Pumla Gobodo-Madikizela, "Women's Contributions to South Africa's Truth and Reconciliation Commission," Women Waging Peace Policy Commission, February 2005, 6.

[53] Shireen Hassim, *Women's Organizations and Democracy in South Africa: Contesting Authority* (Madison: The University of Wisconsin Press, 2006), 39, 4.

[54] Afshar, "Women and Wars," 46.

[55] Ibid., 45.

[56] Jacklyn Cock, *Women and War in South Africa* (Cleveland, OH: Pilgrim Press, 1993), 29, 26.

[57] Cock, *Women and War in South Africa*, 27, 30.

[58] Cock, *Women and War in South Africa*, 47, 51.

[59] Hassim, *Women's Organizations and Democracy in South Africa*, 27.

[60] Cock, *Women and War in South Africa*, 154, 152.

[61] Hassim, *Women's Organizations and Democracy in South Africa*, 34.

[62] Anderlini, *Women Building Peace*, 84.

[63] Sumantra Bose, *Contested Lands: Israel-Palestine, Kashmir, Bosnia, Cyprus, and Sri Lanka* (Cambridge, MA: Harvard University Press, 2007), 61. In his description of the period from granting independence until the division of the island, Bose draws a number of interesting parallels to the situation in Northern Ireland, especially in the 1970s when the Catholic/nationalist groups really began much of their armed violence against British rule.

[64] Cynthia Cockburn, *The Line: Women, Partition and the Gender Order in Cyprus* (London: Zed Books, 2004), 9.

[65] Anderlini, *Women Building Peace*, 84.

[66] Joyce Kaufman discussion with "Marie" in Draperstown, Northern Ireland, December 1999.

Chapter 5

Post-Conflict Activism: Women Working for Peace

In this chapter we explore some of the roles that women have played in peacemaking and conflict resolution, from the formal to the informal, feminist, or "motherist."[1] In the previous chapter we noted that women's political activism typically starts during the period of conflict. One of the ways in which women become actively involved during the conflict is by working to resolve or end the conflict. Before they can begin such an endeavor, however, they must first overcome any number of political, structural, social, and cultural barriers. Working for an end to the violent conflict is not enough—women must also be able to participate in the post-conflict reconstruction of the society.

Once again, it is important to remember that what we are looking at is a process in which one phase merges into another. Hence, ensuring peace means more than just working to end the violence that a society experiences. It also means understanding and addressing the underlying causes that led to that violence initially and doing so as part of the conflict resolution/peacemaking and peacebuilding processes. Here, too, the data show that women bring a different perspective to the table and play an especially important role. As Azza Karam points out, "Studies indicate that sustainable peace is one that is supported and consolidated at the grassroots level, whereas a peace negotiated solely among the elite and without the participation of the majority of people, tends to generate a certain degree of instability."[2] In fact, it is necessary to engage women as part of the process of reconstruction following the conflict if the post-conflict peace is to succeed.

Thus, when we talk about women working for peace, we are referring to the processes that start during conflict to bring an end to it, understanding and addressing the underlying causes of the conflict, and working toward the creation of a peaceful post-conflict society. We contend that women are able to accomplish all of these, if they have the opportunity to do so.

The chapter begins with a discussion of understanding what is meant by peace, how it is traditionally defined in the literature, and how its definition may be

87

broadened to include social justice, insecurity in the home, access to education, and so forth. These issues affect women not by virtue of the fact that they are women per se (an essentialist argument), but that women are "positioned differently"[3] than men in society and therefore are likely to have different priorities on what the post-conflict peace should look like. These different priorities, for example, reflect the gender division of labor in society. As Elaine Zuckerman and Marcia Greenberg observe, women focus on the need to reconstruct rural roads so that they have access to markets, schools, water, health facilities, and so forth—what they call essential services. Men tend to focus on the construction of main roads that they need to get to their jobs in the cities. Thus, the kind of peace negotiated tends to reflect the position that men hold in a society, rather than the priorities of women as well.[4]

The next section of the chapter explores women and negotiation for peace, including a discussion of UN resolutions that speak specifically to the need for women's participation in the peace negotiation process and the post-conflict reconstruction of society. The opportunities and obstacles for women's political activism follows this discussion, specifically focused on the types of political activism in which women engage, namely, community-based, informal, and formal political activism. In this section we also address the issue of women excluded from the peace process and how that exclusion is problematic for the society as a whole, if peace is to endure. The chapter then considers the role of women in the post-conflict reconstruction period. We look at the barriers to women's political involvement in the negotiations to end conflict and the post-conflict period, which includes lack of training and the gendered norms of women's appropriate roles and behavior in society. The chapter concludes with a recap of the importance of women's peace activism, particularly as related to social justice, when the conflict ends and the hard work of reconstructing society begins.

Women, Conflict Resolution, and Peace

Clearly, women have an important role to play in bringing a conflict to a close, in negotiating the peace that will end the conflict, in helping to create a social and political structure that will dominate after the conflict ends, and in playing a role in the post-conflict social and political process especially the formal political process, that can help to avoid or avert conflicts in the future. But this begs a number of important and interrelated questions: How can women become more engaged in the peace process? How can women, who have been excluded from the political process, gain both the training for and access to the process? And, once they are included, how can they make their voices heard and their priorities known and accepted?

Chapter 2 discussed the role of structural violence, that is, the inherent inequality often built into the political and social system that privileges some members of the society at the expense of others; this inequality can contribute to the outbreak of violence. When women organize to work for conflict resolution and peace in a society that is deeply divided, "their agenda is far larger than ending the conflict. Rather, it involves fighting to address the underlying structural issues that contributed to the conflict in the first place, and to put into place a more just society that works toward human rights for all."[5] This conclusion was based on our research on women's political activism in the United States, Northern Ireland, former Yugoslavia, and Israel/Palestine, but it can be seen in other cases as well. What this suggests is that in studying women's work for conflict resolution and peace and then their input into the construction of a post-conflict society, we have to begin by looking not only at how they approach the goal of "peace" for a divided nation, but also how they envision the society after the conflict ends. Former US ambassador and peace activist Swanee Hunt writes:

> Around the globe, women play a vital but often unrecognized role in averting violence and resolving conflict. With expertise in grassroots activism, political leadership, investigative journalism, human rights law, military reform, formal and information negotiations, transitional justice and post-conflict reconstruction, these women bring new approaches to the security sphere process. Sustainable peace, and therefore international security, depends on such innovations.[6]

The ability of women to "dialogue across differences,"[7] as Elisabeth Porter asserts, is a common theme in reviewing the abilities that women can bring to the negotiating table, and one that makes it imperative that women play a role in discussions about peace. Furthermore, as Donna Pankhurst speculates, "groups of women often have a stronger commitment to the ending of violence and the maintenance of long term peace than groups of men, and thus constitute a highly motivated and able group of stakeholders for peacebuilding, who nonetheless are often ignored."[8]

Women's participation, according to Bouta et al., increases the likelihood "that major gender issues will be discussed during peace talks and incorporated in peace accords," and "women often introduce other conflict experiences and set different priorities for peace-building and rehabilitation." Women are likely to focus on women's rights issues. Women form coalitions with others "based on women's shared interests that transcend political, ethnic and religious differences, and bringing a better understanding of social justice and gender inequality to peace negotiations."[9] As Karam also observes, a focus on women's issues and interests by women activists does not mean that women are all the same, a monolithic group, but rather that these issues and interests "need to be *prioritized*, not because they are gender-specific, but because they are the basis of the articulation of the needs of any society" (emphasis in original).[10] Swanee Hunt and Cristina Posa offer a blunt warning: "We can ignore women's work as peacemakers, or we can harness its full force across a wide range of activities relevant to the security sphere: bridging the divide between groups in conflict, influencing local security forces, collaborating with international organizations, and seeking political office."[11]

What Is Peace?

Before we can move into a discussion of women's role in peacemaking and conflict resolution, it is important to define the various terms, starting with what we mean by *peace*. At the most simplistic level, the term *peace* can be defined in the negative, that is, the absence of war. However, in looking at issues of conflict and peace from the perspective of their impact on women, it is necessary to broaden the definition significantly. From an academic perspective, V. Spike Peterson and Anne Sisson Runyan look to the period during the Vietnam War and the rise of the subfield of peace studies, which asked what peace is, "because surely it must be more than simply the time between wars."[12] In fact, the peace that emerges when a conflict ends is one that is a gendered peace. A *gendered peace*, according to Pankhurst, is one in which women "suffer a *backlash* against any new-found freedoms, and they are forced 'back' into kitchens and fields" (emphasis in original). The evidence shows that the peace process and newly created constitutions invariably do not address women's needs. Women's rights are limited or even restricted. Rather than a peace that establishes equality, women face discriminatory laws and policies. In most cases, women find it difficult to oppose existing gender relations in the post-conflict period. Instead, after conflict, patriarchal societies are unwilling or unable to accept changed gender roles, changes women may have gained during the conflict. Pankhurst points out, "The ideological rhetoric is often about 'restoring' or 'returning to' something associated with the status quo before the war, even if the change actually undermines women's rights and places women in a situation that is even more disadvantageous than it ever was in the past."[13]

A workshop on peace through human rights and international understanding, held in Ireland in October 1986, included a discussion group built around the question, "What is peace?" The discussion was summarized as follows: "Peace does not mean a lack of conflict—conflict cannot be avoided, but can be resolved. Conflict arises from a fear of losing that in which one has a vested interest. Removal of fear [that is, creation of trust], brings peace."[14] Inger Skjelsbaek refers to the Third World Conference on Women, held in Nairobi in 1985, which arrived at a definition of peace that includes "not only the absence of war, violence and hostilities at the national and international levels but also the enjoyment of economic and social justice and the entire range of human rights and fundamental freedoms with society."[15] And Tami Jacoby draws on a range of feminist authors who "define peace as the elimination of insecurity and danger," and as "'the enjoyment of economic and social justice, equality, and the entire range of human rights and fundamental freedoms,' or relations between peoples based on 'trust, cooperation and recognition of the interdependence and importance of the common good and mutual interests of all peoples.'"[16]

What all these definitions have in common is the broad understanding that peace must be seen as more than the absence of violent conflict, but must also address broad issues such as equality, social justice, and ensuring basic freedoms and fundamental rights for all people in society. While conflict is in many ways unavoidable, it can be addressed before it becomes violent, or resolved through trust and communication. It is this larger understanding of the concept of peace that defines the type of peace for which women strive.

Peace as a "Women's Issue"

According to Peterson and Runyan, women

> have long been involved in analyzing how to stop war and how to create peace, though they have received no attention for these activities in past and most contemporary international relations literature. Instead, their peace efforts have been ignored or trivialized—largely by men who stereotype women as soft-headed, irrational pacifists. This characterization is political because it excludes women's perspectives from the study of war and peace.[17]

Not only are women's perspectives important because women often see issues of war and peace differently from men, but their own experiences with war and conflict, which vary significantly from men's, mean that they have something important to bring to the table in discussions about peace and post-conflict society. For example, as Christine Chinkin and Hilary Charlesworth demonstrate, women's experiences during war include female combatants, women refugees, and women who were raped during war and have small children or are pregnant and thus encounter the enmity of others in their community. Refugee women who return to their homes may have different goals and perceptions about the post-conflict society than those women who did not flee.[18] Whether taking a feminist or a more traditional approach to viewing society, in general, women's perspective tends to be much broader than simply looking at peace as the end of conflict. It includes addressing the underlying causes of the conflict and the needs (access to food, water, education, housing—"family needs"[19]) facing the society when the conflict ends.

Tickner takes on the myth of "the association of women with peace" with its negative connotations, and she warns that "many contemporary feminists see dangers in the continuation of these essentializing myths that can only result in the perpetuation of women's subordination and reinforce dualisms that serve to make men more powerful." Tickner also notes that there is evidence that indicates women's willingness to support "men's" wars.[20] In fact, in our earlier work[21] and also as noted in Chapter 4 herein, there is considerable evidence that some women did support the causes of war in any number of cases. As Laura Sjoberg and Caron Gentry assert, "Women, like men, sometimes see violence as the best means to political ends."[22] There is also at least one example of a woman, Chandrika Bandaranaike Kumaratunga, who started her career working for peace in Sri Lanka, but who then, as president, "metamorphosed from dove to hawk, pledging to wage a 'war for peace.'"[23] Not all women's political activism is in support of the causes of peace and conflict resolution.

While it is indeed true that some women have supported the causes of war and conflict as noted above, there is ample evidence that women have also played important roles in promoting the causes of peace and resolution of conflict in war-torn societies. This activism has taken a number of directions, from informally trying to raise attention to the causes of peace through the creation of groups such as Women in Black, to working actively for peace, to getting a seat at the negotiating table, as was the case with the Northern Ireland Women's Coalition (NIWC). In some cases women took on the causes of peace because as wives and mothers they felt that they were affected directly. Examples of these include Israel's Parents Against Silence and the Vietnam-era US group Another Mother for Peace.[24] While this broad generalization runs the risk of essentializing women's roles as peacemakers, it is also true that that is the way in which many women self-identified. That is, they did not see themselves as feminists or activists, but rather, they describe themselves as wives and mothers who see it as their responsibility to work for peace. In other cases women were overtly feminist and activist in their approach to working for conflict resolution and peace. The important point is that regardless of the particular ideological approach that was taken (i.e., feminist versus motherist, or traditional), the goal was the same, and that is women working actively for peace and the restructuring of society after conflict.

In all cases women became involved with fighting for peace not only because they were affected by war and conflict, but because they often felt that they had a different perspective to bring and role to play, given their different position in society relative to men. One of the givens facing women who sought to get involved with peace negotiations—whether as a form of feminist political action or as a wife or mother engaged in "small p politics"—was how to break into the negotiations, which were generally structured by men, who held the political power, and, even if they could figure out a way to get involved, how to learn how to engage and to be taken seriously in the negotiation process. These were and are serious dilemmas facing all women who seek a seat at the table and who feel that they have something important to contribute to the process. As the case of Bosnian women's peace activism clearly shows, using "gender essentialisms," according to Elissa Helms, "risk[s] closing off women's potential for influence in the formal (male) political sphere." Helms further argues, however, that for these local activists, "given the moral and political climate of postwar Bosnia, this strategy allows women to gain moral and real, though indirect, power with which to achieve their often very political goals."[25]

Clearly, in looking at situations of conflict, there is a broad category of women who responded politically by working for peace. This can be found across a spectrum of countries, conflicts, and circumstances. Perhaps most noted among these groups is Women in Black, which started as a simple form of protest against Israel's occupation of the West Bank and Gaza and as a way to show solidarity with the Palestinian people. The organization grew and spread to other countries, speaking out against violence and injustice. But what is most important and revealing about Women in Black is its desire to reach across communities in the interest of peace and also social justice, and by having women work together *as women* in pursuit of goals for the common good. Further, although it started in response to a specific event, the mandate of the group has expanded, and according to its website, it has become "a world-wide network of women committed to peace with justice and actively opposed to injustice, war, militarism and other forms of violence."

According to its website, "'Women in Black' was inspired by earlier movements of women who demonstrated on the streets, making a public space for women to be heard—particularly Black Sash, in South Africa, and the Madres de la [Mothers of the] Plaza de Mayo, seeking the 'disappeared' in the political repression in Argentina." Formed in 1955 in South Africa, Black Sash predated Women in Black by decades and brought together white and black women in support of the struggle against apartheid. The black sashes, "worn in mourning at the death of constitutional rights," according to the Black Sash website, were a symbol of what the wearers saw as the erosion of the rule of law. Although it was initially created as an organization of white women, Mary Burton, a representative of the Black Sash, found that "there was 'a sense of urgency' to unite women across racial and ideological spheres and that 'our identity as women provides us with one common bond that may help us transcend the [barriers and divisions].'"[26] Thus, their role as women was one thing that brought together a range of people who were united in their common desire to make sure that their voices were heard on important matters of politics and social justice.

Like the better-known Argentine group Mothers of the Plaza de Mayo, motherhood as a central identity brought the women of Black Sash together. According to Jacklyn Cock, what this organization and another, the Detainees Parents Support Committee, did in South Africa was force the state to confront "new forms of resistance based on notions of motherhood, parenthood, and the family. Many of the activists were not initially mobilized by ideology, but by the detention of a relative and the destruction of the family. In this sense, the war *politicized* the traditional role of women within the family, and family relationships proved to be important in mobilizing women" (emphasis added).[27] Hence, motherhood played a mobilizing role for women against apartheid and the status quo in South Africa and against the regime in Argentina.

Bosnian women's NGOs also serve as an example of women's groups who "consciously embrace this association of women with home, motherhood, and nonparticipation in 'politics,'" according to Helms. Focused on ethnic reconciliation and assisting returning refugees in the post-conflict environment, for these organizations, motherhood is "the defining feature of women's peacemaking roles."[28]

In looking at women's activism for peace, then, one of the first questions that can be asked is how women were able to bridge the divide or move past the divisions that separated their country, sometimes violently. The easiest answer is that women could do this because of the common threads that they saw uniting them. Hence, rather than focusing on the factors that separate groups—ethnic, religious, national, tribal, and so on—women were (and are) able to see all the issues that held them together. For example, as illustrated by the examples above, women were united in their traditional roles as wives and mothers, which served as a common bond. They were bound together in their opposition to rape and other forms of violence against women that increase during times of conflict and war. They were opposed to discrimination against women, and they favored social justice and equality. They were often brought together by a common desire to improve the situation within their own communities, which is an area over which they felt they could have some impact. They were united in their common desire to knit together a social fabric that has been torn apart by war, and to do so in a way that would minimize the risk of violence in the future. And often, they realized that as wives and mothers they had common ideas and dreams, among them, the elimination of violence that was destroying their families.

Of course, it is important to reiterate that not all women felt or feel this way, nor could all women transcend the differences that ripped their country/society/culture apart. However, for those who could, these are some of the reasons why. It is in understanding those reasons that it is also possible to address better how, when, and why women choose to work for peace, often against great social and political odds.

Women and Negotiations for Peace

Peace, or the cessation of hostilities, can be the result of direct negotiations between the belligerents or, in what has become the more common approach, discussions can be facilitated by a third-party mediator. This can be another country (represented by a high-ranking diplomat of a country not directly involved in the conflict) or an international organization, such as the United Nations. Third-party mediation has a number of advantages. As Sumantra Bose notes in the case of the Sri Lanka peace process, "At the minimum, the internationalization of the peace process—the central and direct role of Norway, and the less direct involvement of the United States, Japan, and the European Union—has made a total breakdown and resumption of full-scale war significantly less likely than it would be otherwise."[29] By bringing members of the international community into the process, the profile of the negotiations is raised, and success, or the risk of failure, becomes highly politicized. Thus, the stakes for resuming or increasing violence are higher for all the parties, who then become more willing to talk.

As we use them, the terms *conflict resolution, peacemaking,* and *peace negotiations* are very similar; all deal with ending a conflict, including negotiations for an agreement to bring peace to a divided country. A UN Expert Group Meeting held in the Dominican Republic in October 1996 on the impact of gender differences on political decision-making and conflict resolution recognized that "peacemaking may well include the forceful stoppage of violence but also that, without negotiation over the real issues underlying the conflict, such 'peace' will not be more than temporary."[30] Hence, these broad categories all require a *process* of discussion that assumes (1) the parties are negotiating in good faith, (2) there is a frank exchange of ideas, a willingness to address the issues that led to the conflict, and (3) there is an understanding of the need to compromise in the interest of the greater good.

One aspect of the negotiation process leading to peace or the resolution of a conflict involves determining how to reconstruct or rebuild the society after the conflict ends, and how to do so in a way that minimizes the prospect of ongoing or further conflict. This suggests that one of the components of conflict resolution or peace negotiations must be an outline of the reconstruction of society in a way that furthers the goals of peace, such as making sure that there is equality or at least equal opportunity for all, a guarantee of basic human rights, and full and open access to the political system. Again, the expert group referred to above concluded that it is important to broaden "the peace-building approach so that it prevents the outbreak of violent conflict by removing or at least reducing the fundamental causes of the conflict."[31] This goal can best be achieved—perhaps can only be achieved— if all constituencies are represented at the table. This, too, argues for the inclusion of women as participants.

Northern Ireland, specifically the negotiations surrounding the 1998 Good Friday Agreement and the creation of the NIWC represents a case in point. The historic agreement was the culmination of formal negotiations to end the Troubles. The process of negotiating an end to the most recent three decades of violence was long and not always easy.[32] One of the issues surrounding the negotiations was who would be invited to sit at the table and to take part in the actual discussions. This was important to many women, who had not only been directly affected by the violence but who also wanted to have input into the discussions about what the society would look like after the period of violence officially ended. They needed to be represented at the talks so that women's perspectives and issues (that is, social justice issues, including gender equality) could become part of the conversation. NIWC was created specifically to give women a seat at the table and a voice in the negotiations, and two women did get the votes to participate in the negotiations.[33]

Yet, despite its success in getting to the table, the NIWC was formally disbanded in May 2006, following a number of years in which the party could no longer get representatives elected to office. In many ways the perception of the general public, which had supported the NIWC earlier, seemed to be that with the end of the Troubles, the work of the party was done. Nonetheless, in its report disbanding the NIWC, among the items identified that still remained to be accomplished was the "need to convince government/public of particular value of women's engagement in political/public life," and the need for "more women in public and political life—need a radical policy change to create a critical mass."[34] Clearly, the NIWC made a difference in the outcome of the negotiations but was unsuccessful in accomplishing all of its larger goals regarding women's active participation in the political process.

While we can focus on the value added by women's participation in negotiations, it is also possible to look at the ways in which peace talks are diminished by the *absence* of women, especially when it comes to using those negotiations to help construct or reconstruct the society that will exist after conflict ends (a point we will address in more detail below). As Bouta, Frerks, and Bannon note in their study, "Without a voice, women's concerns are neither prioritized nor resourced."[35] Although women's presence at peace talks will not guarantee that gender equity or social justice issues will be raised, it is possible to conclude that they will *not* be raised unless women are represented in the negotiations.

For women, then, the real question is how to become involved in the negotiations to end a conflict and thereby assure that they have input into the post-conflict structure of society. It is in recognizing this critical need for women to be represented at the negotiating table that the United Nations passed Resolution 1325, an important document that highlights the importance of women's participation and input at the peace negotiations and peacebuilding stage.

UN Resolutions and Women's Participation in the Peace Process

On October 31, 2000, the United Nations Security Council adopted Resolution 1325 on Women, Peace, and Security in recognition both of the toll that war and conflict take on women and of the contributions that women can make to the conflict resolution and peace process. According to Cockburn, "Resolution 1325 may well be the only Security Council resolution for which the groundwork, the diplomacy and lobbying, the drafting and redrafting, was almost entirely the work of civil society, and certainly the first in which the actors were almost all women."[36] Resolution 1325 grew out of the need to implement some of the initiatives put forward at the Beijing Conference five years earlier. The Beijing Platform for Action (PFA) noted twelve "critical areas of concern" that hindered women's advancement. According to Elisabeth Porter, "the PFA represents a strong statement of international commitment to the goals of gender equality, development and peace, and the full realization of rights and freedom for women." The PFA paved the way for NGOs to pursue issues of gender equality at the international level. Pushed by NGOs and with the support of a number of sympathetic officials, UN Security Council Resolution 1325 was debated and then passed. This was the first time that the Security Council "discussed women in their own right in relation to peace and security. It is also the first time that the Security Council officially endorsed civil society groups, especially women in the peace process."[37] Thus the resolution was seen as important in the effort to inject women into the processes of conflict resolution, peace negotiations, and peacebuilding. Resolution 1325 itself makes clear "the important role of women in the prevention and resolution of conflicts and in peace-building, . . . and the need to increase their role in decision-making with regard to conflict prevention and resolution."

While this resolution was hailed as an important step forward for women internationally, the reality is that implementing this resolution has been difficult. Or, as Margaret Ward observes,

> while Resolution 1325 provides for women's voices to be heard, it does not emphasize their role as agents of social change but merely reiterates the importance of their participation for the maintenance of peace and security. Therefore, while women are being included within organizations, they remain mere token presences. Increasingly, they are making it plain that much more will be necessary before women can effect meaningful change in society.[38]

Sudan is a case in point. The civil war in Sudan lasted twenty-two years (1983–2005), culminating in a peace agreement that ended the conflict among several rebel groups (including the Sudan People's Liberation Movement/Army, or SPLM/A) and the government. The impact of the civil war on women has been clear. Women were both victims (of sexual violence and rape, for example) and agents (as combatants). Women formed networks of peace activists, such as the Sudanese Women's Vote for Peace and the New Sudan Women's Association, with the goal of ending the conflict and rebuilding society. Two demands were essential to these women's groups. First, they sought an end to the conflict. Second, they demanded that women be included in the formal peace talks (called for by UN Security Council Resolution 1325). A few women were nominated by the SPLA to serve as delegates to the 2002 Machakos talks. The participation of these women was not significant, however, because the women were added at the last minute to the delegations involved in the talks. They were then unable to consult with one other and thus could not "develop a coherent women's agenda." As a result, the Comprehensive Peace Agreement (CPA) does not include many provisions related to women and girls.[39] In essence, these women were tokens.

Since the passage of Resolution 1325, the UN has continued to promote the idea of women's participation in the peace process and post-conflict reconstruction. For example, the UN has attempted to increase the number of women participating in its peacekeeping operations. In doing so, the UN hopes that these women can serve as a positive role model to local women. Moreover, the UN recognizes that having more women represented within its organization may increase the possibility that local women will be included in the formal peace talks, given that the UN views its peacebuilding and peace talks as very much a component of the "formal peace processes."[40] And yet, as Porter shows, in October 2002, UN peacekeeping operations in fifteen countries had no women in their missions. There may have been gender advisers (Democratic Republic of Congo, Bosnia, and East Timor, for example) or gender units (Kosovo and East Timor), but no women serving in those peacekeeping operations.[41]

As discussed in Chapter 3, UN Security Council Resolution 1820 (2008) calls for an end to sexual violence against civilians in war. The resolution also affirms "the important role of women in the prevention and resolution of conflicts and in peacebuilding, and *stressing* the importance of their equal participation and full involvement in all efforts for the maintenance and promotion of peace and security, and the need to increase their role in decision-making with regard to conflict prevention and resolution" (emphasis in original). The resolution also noted its concerns regarding "the persistent obstacles and challenges to women's participation and full involvement in the prevention and resolution of conflicts as a result of violence, intimidation and discrimination, which erode women's capacity and legitimacy to participate in post-conflict public life." The resolution continues by "acknowledging the negative impact this has on durable peace, security and reconciliation, including post-conflict peacebuilding."[42]

UN Security Council resolution 1820 was followed by Resolutions 1888 and 1889 in 2009. While Resolution 1888 focused on the issue of sexual violence against women and girls in conflict, the resolution also reaffirmed commitment to Resolution 1325, specifically, the concern about "the underrepresentation of women in formal peace processes." The resolution also recognized "that the promotion and empowerment of women and that support for women's organizations and networks are essential in the consolidation of peace to promote the equal and full participation of women."[43] Resolution 1889 also reaffirmed the Security Council's commitment to Resolution 1325, "*Reiterating* the need for the full, equal and effective participation of women at all stages of peace processes given their vital role in the prevention and resolution of conflict and peacebuilding, *reaffirming* the key role women can play in reestablishing the fabric of society and stressing the need for their involvement in the development and implementation of post-conflict strategies in order to take into account their perspectives and needs" (emphasis in original). As with other resolutions, 1889 also expressed concern that women continue to be underrepresented at all stages of the peace processes, noting their small numbers at the formal political levels, both at the mediation talks and high decision-making levels. The resolution also stressed the particular needs of women and that those needs should be reflected in the peacemaking and peacebuilding periods, namely, their "physical security, health services including reproductive and mental health, ways to ensure their livelihoods, land and property rights, employment."[44]

Despite the passage of Resolutions 1325, 1820, 1888, and 1889, and the recognition of what women can bring to the negotiating table, the reality is that there are few women involved in such endeavors.[45] As Porter argues, "What United Nations recommendations still miss is that many women are already involved in community groups. Their political skills are not recognized, and they are not harnessed in more formal political arenas."[46] Thus, one could argue that there are many reasons for the underrepresentation of women in the peace process. Anderlini points out that "the paucity of women in leadership positions in political parties, the state, or nonstate groups is perhaps the most pertinent reason for their absence from peace talks." Although women held leadership positions in the government as well as opposition groups, in several conflicts (El Salvador, Sri Lanka, and Uganda for example) they were not found in high level decision-making positions. Given that the women were not included in these high level positions, it is not surprising that they were then excluded from the peace talks.[47] And, of course, many of the women who mobilized or became politically active during a conflict did not see their actions as overtly political, which further removed them from participating in the formal political process or from remaining part of the political process after the conflict ended.

Yet, the inclusion of women significantly alters the dynamics of the peace process itself, as well as in preparing for the society that will follow. Porter also makes clear that the inclusion of women in peace negotiations matters for the "democratic legitimacy of the process." Women's participation is necessary because the peace process is then "more responsive to the priorities of all affected citizens."[48] The challenge for women, and also the men involved, is how to include women and ensure that their voices will be heard and their ideas taken seriously. As demonstrated in the next section, women bring skills they have cultivated and developed from their work at the community and grassroots levels, and often honed during conflict, that can be of importance in the post-conflict peace talks and the peacebuilding that ensues after the fighting is over.

Women's Political Activism and Peace: Opportunities and Obstacles

There are many reasons for women to be involved with negotiations to resolve or end a conflict. Yet those at the peace negotiations are mostly men, the "male representatives of the fighting parties, concentrating on negotiating an end to war." Getting a sustainable peace means women's experiences must be included.[49] Thus, the best way to prepare for the peace is to ensure inclusion in the negotiations to resolve the conflicts that start during war. And inclusion requires that women have a seat at the table.

Hunt asks rhetorically, "Why Women?" and proceeds to answer that question using a number of criteria: *fairness*, in that "women account for half the population and therefore it's only fair that they comprise half the decision-makers." She speaks of *compensation*, specifically given "how greatly women have been victimized, they deserve to be heard." There is the issue of *representation*, "leaving women out of the peacemaking process means their concerns are likely to be ignored or bargained away in the negotiation process." And she notes the "*efficiency* argument," that is, for lasting stability "we need peace promoters, not just warriors, at the table. More often than not, those peace promoters are women." She also reminds us that "a negotiated settlement must have the buy-in of the masses before it is truly sustainable, and thus stakeholders from throughout the society must be involved in the informal and formal peace process" (emphasis in original).[50] Women thus have a vested interest in assuring the establishment of a just and lasting peace, and the most effective way that they can achieve that goal is to work for peace and, whenever possible, participate in the negotiations themselves.

Who are the women who actually do get to sit at the table, where do they come from, and how did they get there? As Anderlini notes in a study for the UN Development Fund for Women, "women are more likely than men to have arrived via civil activism, often with first-hand experience of the brutal consequences of conflict."[51] Furthermore, the women who are willing to make the effort to get involved with peace negotiations do so because they see the personal impact of the outcomes, not necessarily because they want to benefit personally from the result of the negotiations. Or, to quote Palestinian Authority spokesperson Hanan Ashrawi, although women "bear the brunt, they pay the price, they don't always reap the rewards. The rewards are for the men; the consequences are for the women."[52]

Women have a long history of working for peace. In the United States, the International Alliance of Women was established as part of the National American Women Suffrage Association. Meeting in 1902, before women had the vote, the group's objectives were "to urge women to use their rights and influence public life to ensure that the status of every individual, without distinction of sex, race or creed, shall be based on respect for human personality, the only guarantee for individual freedom."[53] A second meeting was held in Berlin in 1904, and the organization was expanded to become the International Woman Suffrage Alliance. The group continued to meet regularly until the outbreak of the First World War, although "members' opinions were divided over the issue of pacifism, which led to the creation of another body, the Women's International League for Peace and Freedom in 1915."[54]

An International Conference of Women convened at The Hague in 1915 "called for mediation to end the war." As Joshua Goldstein notes, when the United States entered the First World War, "some feminists remained antiwar activists, but faced considerable challenges as most of their colleagues supported the war effort."[55] Many felt that it would be unpatriotic to question the war. Jane Addams led the effort in opposition to the war, and she believed that "mothers would be the first to protest the slaughter of their children in war, and that 'women of civilization' [women from the United States] could help end this senseless killing." However, Addams also believed that not only women felt this way, but that men did as well.[56] Although Addams was branded a traitor by some women for her point of view, she won the Nobel Peace Prize in 1931.

There are a number of things that are instructive about these early examples of women's political activism for peace, which all grew out of a larger movement for women's suffrage, which was a critical step toward guaranteeing full equality for women as well as access to the political system. Further, part of the stated goal of these women's organizations was to work and strive for broad social justice issues, such as guaranteeing basic rights for all. This theme would continue to the present. Finally, it is clear that there was not one single point of view held by all women. Rather, the women in these groups were divided in their support for or opposition to the war, and all for good reasons.

It is also important to remember that at that time, since women did not have the vote, the only way in which they could try to influence the political decision-makers on grave matters such as war and peace was to organize and try to bring pressure to bear. Clearly, the tradition of women organizing outside the political system to try to influence the outcome of events has a long history. But an important question to explore is why some women continued to choose the indirect path rather than working within the political system, even after they got the vote and could become "equal" members of the political system as well as decision-makers themselves.

Recognizing the role that women can and need to play not only in resolving conflict but in helping to create or construct a post-conflict society that will be less violence prone, the issue is how to get more women to the table. Here the examples show that women have followed a broad range of approaches (community-based activism, informal and formal political activism), from those that are overtly feminist to pursuing a strategy tied to women's more traditional roles as wives and mothers. Some of the choices depended upon the options available to the women as well as their own perspectives on what approach would be most effective.

Women and Community-based Activism: A Step Toward Working for Peace

Women's political activism involves the process by which women move from the private sphere to engage with the public, which has generally been seen as the male domain. Often the safest and least threatening way for both women and the men around them to engage politically is to start in their community. This also ensures that local concerns are raised and, hopefully, met. These concerns are especially important when women are working for peace or conflict resolution. Work at the community, or grassroots, level provides an important starting point and basis for cohesion among women who have similar concerns and attitudes. As noted in the report by the Northern Ireland Voluntary Trust, a nonprofit charity whose mission is to fund and support community activism, "Local community activism is the most usual starting point for women engaging in public life—with 'campaigns around local issues often helping to galvanize women.' This can in turn play an important role in politicizing women."[57]

According to Bouta, Frerks, and Bannon women's organizations "form an essential part of civil society and have the potential to promote women's leadership, to build awareness of women's rights, and to contribute to gender equality.[58] Women's organizations, often community based, can play an important role in politicizing and galvanizing women as well as helping them overcome many of the structural barriers that impede their broader involvement in the political system. In addition, many of these community-based organizations, which allow women to work across divides in societies in conflict, can also provide the first step toward women working for peace.

A UN Expert Group Meeting addressed the relationship between community-based activism and the larger peace process. It concluded: "There should be greater involvement of women at the grassroots level in conflict resolution and the peace process. This will ensure that the drafting of peace agreements reflect gender concerns." The report states that women "from the locality should be involved in identifying problems, and in designing and implementing solutions as a means of more effective development of local confidence building measures."[59]

But this approach carries with it some dangers. As Porter states, "Unless we see the boundary shift from exclusive views of citizenship as a relationship between the state and its subjects towards the inclusion of political spaces such as women's community activism, much of women's political activity goes theoretically unrecognized and practically undervalued."[60] Thus there is an extra burden on women who engage politically. Not only do they have to establish themselves and their credibility, but once they start moving beyond the areas that have been the traditional domain of women (such as education, health, and domestic violence) and into the male areas such as conflict resolution, the burden really is on them to prove themselves.

Monica McWilliams, one of the two women elected to represent the Northern Ireland Women's Coalition at the Northern Ireland peace talks, wrote in 1995 about women's activism in Northern Ireland. She identified what she saw as five stages of women's involvement. To some extent, this was chronological, but the progression documents how women became more political and politicized over time and with the acceleration of political violence. In her assessment women's political activism in Northern Ireland was tied to the larger civil rights movements of the 1960s and 1970s, through the feminist struggles of the 1970s and 1980s, and then to "the recent campaigns by women's groups as they struggle for increased recognition in the new peace processes which may determine the political future of Northern Ireland."[61] In other words, she describes a process of growing involvement by women starting within a broader (civil rights) movement and then building with the underlying goal being that of making the society a better place. What is especially instructive about the continuum that she defines is that it can be applied more generally to women's political activism beyond Northern Ireland.

Porter approaches women's political activism slightly differently. She identifies a number of reasons the community is a safe place for women's political activism to begin. She sees community as essential to the lived experiences of national identity as they occur in the political, economic, cultural, and social dynamics of people's narratives. It is these locations that "open the political space to where women's activism lies."[62] Although the type of activism that women might engage in within the community may be of a limited nature and often tied to "women's issues," such as rape counseling, education, welfare rights, education, and child care, it gives women the experience of organizing and uniting for a common cause, often among groups that would otherwise be in conflict. With participation in grassroots activism women also gain leadership skills. Furthermore, it is this community-based activism that often provides the common basis for women working across divisions for peace.

The example of "Audrey," a woman community activist based in Shankill in the heart of the Protestant community, is instructive. Audrey works with women in the areas of sports and physical activity. She became involved with cross-community work when she participated with a group of women who went on an outing together to climb a mountain; they needed to help one another in order to succeed. She saw the religious divide clearly when her brother married a Catholic woman, and neither she, nor others in her family, attended. She has been estranged from her brother since, to her regret now.

Her subsequent experiences working with women across the communities were so positive that she has remained involved with women's sports and physical activity as a way to unite Catholic and Protestant women in pursuit of common goals. She acknowledges that there is bitterness on both sides, and that both feel betrayed by the terms of the Belfast (Good Friday) Agreement. But she also speaks for many women when she says that she has learned a great deal from her own experiences, which have resulted in fostering understanding across the religious divide.

Joyce Kaufman, meeting with Audrey, Women in Sports and Physical Activity; Clare, Sports Development Officer; and Robert, Community Sports Development Officer for Northern Belfast, on November 20, 2007. Both Audrey and Robert are Protestant, while Clare is Catholic. In the conversation with them, one of the things that they talked about was their ability to work together and to learn from one another, something that had earlier been antithetical to all of them.

Women's political activism starting in and based in the community is a pattern that can be seen across a range of countries. Shireen Hassim, writing about women's organizations in South Africa, notes much the same pattern identified above in the case of Northern Ireland. In South Africa, "the everyday organization of women around their role as mothers and community members far outweighs the number of women engaged in overt political activities." The "new democracy," as Hassim calls it, which has emerged in South Africa since apartheid "has opened the possibilities for women's organizations to take up issues that are outside the conventional definitions of political action and to demand attention by the state to issues that states have generally been reluctant to regulate (that is, regulating and mitigating men's power in the private sphere)."[63]

Women Working Outside the System—Informal Political Activism

Peace negotiations, of course, exist within the purview of the formal political system. Ideally, the best way to ensure women's input is to have a seat at the table at which peace is being negotiated and conflict resolved. Realistically, this option is not usually open to women. Participants generally include the decision-makers, augmented by the leaders of relevant informal groups—namely, men. The patriarchal nature of these organizations means that women are routinely excluded from the process unless they can find a way to insert themselves into it. And, even if they are able to do so, there are no guarantees that they can make their voices heard. Therefore, in many cases women start working for peace informally, long before the formal negotiations actually begin. Thus, when we talk about women working for peace, we need to subdivide the category still further into women who work for peace through various groups, such as NGOs or informal organizations that exist outside the system, versus those who manage somehow to get a seat at the table and participate in direct, formal negotiations. It is instructive to look at examples of each to examine what their goals were, and whether they were achieved.

If one subscribes to the concept that the process of building a sustainable peace "involves the whole country and especially the state, it has to be built by civil society *from the bottom up*" (emphasis added).[64] This, in turn, requires involvement of all those people who are affected by the conflict. There is ample evidence supporting the critical role that women have played at the community or grassroots level to work for peace, as noted in the previous section. It is here that women's groups or organizations can be most effective, often because these women were directly touched by the violence.[65] For example, in northeast India the Naga women have been mediating in conflicts that date back centuries. The Naga Mothers' Association (NMA), which was formed in 1984, "draws on traditional identities of women as peacemakers, to assert their role as arbiters and mediators, expanding the middle ground for peace. On the other hand, the Naga Women's Union of Manipur (NWUM), formed in 1994 in preparation for the Fourth World Conference in Beijing, asserts women's rights more broadly." These two groups, with different ideological backgrounds and orientations, "work symbiotically, advocating the message of peace, diffusing tensions, reconciling warring parties, and drawing on their distinct identities and constituencies to maximize effect."[66]

In Israel there are a number of examples of grassroots organizations that were organized specifically to work for peace and for issues of social justice, especially for the Palestinians. The Intifada of 1987 was a galvanizing event that resulted in the emergence and growth of a number of women's organizations. It was in that context that Women in Black was born. In addition, there were other groups, including Israeli Women Against the Occupation [of the West Bank and Gaza Strip], a national Women and Peace Coalition, and Israel Women's Peace Net (Reshet). All were formed within the two years following the Intifada. All of these looked at the issue of peace from a broad social and political perspective, and involved direct interaction between Israeli and Palestinian women. It is important to note that despite the fact that women activists were working for peace at a grassroots level in Israel for more than a decade prior to the Oslo process that led to the signing of the

Declaration of Principles between Israel and the Palestinian Liberation Organization (PLO) in 1993, "women were largely excluded from the formal political and diplomatic negotiations between Israel and the PLO. . . . Despite all their work for peace, since women were not well-represented in the political system and, in fact, had been systematically excluded from it, they were not part of the formal discussions surrounding the peace process."[67]

Women have to learn how to get involved if they are to overcome the many structural barriers that are imposed upon them. This is part of the process of educating women about the political system and the ways in which they can make a difference. For example, in the 1970s and 1980s, the International Alliance of Women sponsored a series of conferences and seminars in different regions all dealing with women's contributions to peace and understanding.[68] In most cases the focus was on women making a difference at the grassroots level with the acknowledgment that governments *should* recognize the role that these women activists play. However, acknowledging the political reality, in most cases the seminars also recognized how important it is for women to work together to bring pressure on their governments in order to ensure that women have access to decision-making bodies, and that their voices are heard on matters of importance to their society, including issues of war and peace. The participants were primarily community-based activists who wanted to learn more about and share ways in which they could have a greater role in their society. While not all of the seminars were geared toward working for peace per se, what they all had in common was a stress on the ways in which women can work together to build trust that can ensure a more peaceful and equal society.

In looking at informal peace activism, and negotiations in particular, a choice or decision that women make is the particular approach that they will take to the negotiations. Specifically, one option is whether to take an overtly feminist stance or to work for peace as wives or mothers, that is, employing a more traditional perspective. Rather than looking at the latter (traditional) as less important or significant than the former (feminist), a more traditional approach often affords women the access that they might have been denied otherwise. In fact, it provides an important common theme that brings women together and, in some societies, elevates their importance. In some cases women feel that they do not have a choice; they become active politically because they or a member of their family was directly affected by the violence and the conflict, and so they respond in the way that they know best, as wives or mothers who are working for peace. Moreover, in many cases where women are working within the bounds of a traditional patriarchal structure, they have to navigate the barriers that have been imposed if they are going to have any input at all.

An important point to consider is whether women's organizations should remain engaged in informal negotiations and political activism or enter into the formal political process. As noted in Chapter 2, feminist women's groups often choose to remain outside the formal political process, thereby maintaining their autonomy. In maintaining autonomy, in the case of Latin American feminist organizations promoting democratization and human rights, these organizations are able to avoid corruption and dependence on the state.[69] As will be shown in the next section, it is generally recognized that women's participation at the formal negotiations is necessary to ensure that women's voices are heard and their issues brought to the table. Moreover, feminist scholars claim that without women's participation and representation "existing patterns of entrenched masculinity are highly *unlikely* to change," thus reinforcing the existing gendered power structures.[70]

Women Working for Peace Within the System—Formal Negotiations

For the host of reasons noted above, women are often more active and successful working within the informal peace processes, or working outside the formal political structure to exert pressure on it, than they are working within and being part of the formal process (the obstacles to women's participation will be discussed in a subsequent section). However, unless women are represented at the table, it is unlikely that "women's issues" will be raised at all. Moreover, as Anderlini makes clear, the peace negotiations will occur whether women and civil society groups are there or not in support of the process.[71] Thus, only by having women sitting at the formal negotiating table is there any guarantee that the agenda that many women would like to pursue both in ending the conflict and in restructuring and rebuilding the society after the conflict will be put forward. Furthermore, as Bouta, Frerks, and Bannon note, it should not be assumed that "women's presence in the peace process will guarantee that gender equality issues will be on the agenda." They give the example of the negotiations in El Salvador where, although "nearly one-third of the FMLN negotiators were women, gender equality was not incorporated in El Salvador's peace agreements, which even included some discriminatory provisions against women."[72]

There are numerous examples of women who participated directly in peace and/ or conflict resolution negotiations despite the many barriers to their participation. Anderlini notes that South African women "were important to the process. They were pivotal to the entire anti-apartheid movement and transition to peace." She continues, "Though women were underrepresented on the local peace committees, South African and UN personnel noted the qualitative difference that women peace monitors made in enabling access to and fostering trust within communities."[73] Although Anderlini also points out that much about the South African situation was unique, it is also "one of few models of integrated conflict prevention and nonviolent transformation work in practice. . . . Even though it cannot be replicated overnight in another context, the lessons and experience should be effectively captured or integrated into international conflict prevention practice."[74] Nonetheless, the lessons of South Africa are instructive and can be exported to other cases. For example, there are strong ties between women in South Africa and those in Northern Ireland, and the latter benefited from the lessons of the former.[75]

In Anderlini's assessment, one of the most important lessons that can be drawn from South Africa and other cases is "the notion of community involvement and inclusiveness that gives the silent majority of peace supporters a voice needs to be more systematically and widely embraced."[76] And these are characteristics that women bring—and have brought—to peace negotiations.

In another example, in Guyana, starting in 2002, the United Nations "tackled issues of social tension, primarily between Indo-Guyanese and Afro-Guyanese, and sought to correct deficiencies in electoral strategy to quell potential violence in the 2006 elections." According to Anderlini, a partnership program was put into place under the overall umbrella of a Social Cohesion Program. "They worked with women's, youth, and media groups to mitigate politically driven tensions between the communities and promote peacebuilding in the run-up to parliamentary elections." She also gives the example of how the United Nations Department of Political Affairs worked "directly with a regional women's peace network . . . to prevent the spread of conflict across Sierra Leone, Liberia and Guinea."[77]

These are all positive examples of the ways in which women and women's groups can be integrated into the conflict resolution and peace negotiation process. But these are also anecdotal and do not necessarily reflect the norm. In fact, the norm is that despite UN Resolutions 1325 and 1889, and other conscious efforts to include women in the peace process, they largely remain apart from it in most cases.

The Northern Ireland Women's Coalition: A Case Study of Women's Political Activism

The necessity to include women raises two important questions: How can women become more engaged in the peace process? and, How can they make their voices heard? Here the case of the NIWC is instructive.[78]

The NIWC was created in 1996 specifically to find a way to ensure that women had input at the then-upcoming All-Party (Peace) Talks. Women political activists were aware that the only way women would be represented at the talks would be if they were elected. In effect, they had six weeks "in which to form a new political party, to gather a representative body of women together, to get some of them to put their names forward, to submit all the necessary paperwork—and not forgetting having to run an election. We had no money, no offices, no premises, and we only had one or two individuals among us who had more than a passing idea as to how we should go about all this."[79] To read about what it took to ensure that the Women's Coalition had its two delegates (Monica McWilliams and Pearl Sagar) elected is a study in grassroots political activism. Against all odds, the coalition did succeed, and the two women were elected to represent the NIWC at the peace talks that eventually led to the Belfast (Good Friday) Agreement. Its success was due, in part, to the fact that "the NIWC had remained true to its genuine cross-community ethos, pioneering the path that others will have to follow. Both communities responded to the appeal of the NIWC, and rewarded them accordingly."[80]

However, getting elected and being taken seriously were not the same. The story of the team of women from the NIWC who participated in the peace talks themselves as well as the various events surrounding the actual talks was a study in frustration. As Baroness May Blood, one of the founders of the NIWC and an important participant in the talks process, describes it: "The reaction from some of the male politicians in the mainstream Unionist parties to our two Women's Coalition representatives was astonishing. Monica and Pearl went through totally unacceptable abuse at their hands."[81] Although the women were able to devise a plan that resulted in minimizing the abuse, it did not stop all together.

What was most important, though, was that creating the NIWC was a way to achieve a goal, "which was to make sure that women were represented at the talks table. After all, women represented fifty-two per cent of the population of Northern Ireland, and if there were going to be important talks about this society's future, then women should be included."[82] And the two representatives of the NIWC were the only women at the peace table.

By all accounts, the women's presence was felt not only in the issues that they raised but in the process by which they did so. According to Bronagh Hinds, who was one of the founders of the NIWC and then served as election manager in 1996, the members of the Women's Coalition approached the talks in a way that differed from their male counterparts. They believed strongly that all parties had to be included in the talks and that all stakeholders had to be at the table, and that this approach was consistent with the core values of equality, human rights, and inclusion that the group advocated. Further, their approach to the negotiations themselves differed from that of many of the men around the table; they preferred to create an environment within which it was possible to air all positions and points of view. This inclusive approach proved to be effective and allowed the members of the NIWC to meet with and discuss various points of view with the other delegates at times, helping to move the discussion forward.[83]

It is very possible that the peace talks would have been successful without the presence of the women from the NIWC, but we will not know that. What we do know is that their participation did have a positive impact. But for every case of Northern Ireland or South Africa, there is an example of Bosnia, where not only were women not represented at the peace negotiations, but their point of view was not injected either.

According to former senator George Mitchell, who chaired the Northern Ireland Peace Talks, the presence of the NIWC was important. In an email response to questions posed by the authors specifically about the role of the NIWC, he supported Hinds's assessment when he wrote that "the Coalition played a significant and positive role in the talks. They were a constant voice of reason and moderation." He also added that because of the number of actors involved (two governments and ten political parties), "it's difficult to assess precisely cause and effect in the dynamics. But I have no doubt that the Coalition contributed to the favorable result.

Email from Senator Mitchell to Joyce Kaufman, August 30, 2007, sent in response to her questions about the role of women in general, and the NIWC in particular, at the Peace Talks.

Women Excluded from the Peace Process

The Dayton Peace Accords that ended the war in Bosnia is an example of the ways in which peace agreements are gendered both in their exclusion of women from the actual negotiations and in their failure to recognize women's needs in the post-conflict society.[84] The Kvinna till Kvinna Foundation, based in Stockholm, produced a report on the gender aspect in the Dayton Peace Accords. In this particular case, it identified "the lack of gender awareness among senior staff within the international community. The Dayton Peace Accords put very little emphasis on the importance of civil society organizations, such as women's NGOs, and their potential contribution to peace-building and structural stability."[85] Thus, the potential contribution that women could make to the actual negotiations was not considered nor was it reflected in the makeup of the negotiating teams.

Yet, as the Kvinna till Kvinna report notes, in the case of the war in Bosnia, "civil society, including women's international and local organizations, has exerted enormous energy to alleviate the consequences of conflict (already during the war), rebuild a war-torn society, maintain dialogue across ethnic lines, contribution to the consolidation of peace, i.e., the establishment of democratic social structures and monitoring mechanisms." And, given the contributions that women make (often through NGOs), the knowledge and experience that is accumulated "accelerates the work for sustainable and democratic post-war societies . . . [and] is a valuable contribution that should not be ignored." Conversely, "If these factors are left out, sustainable peace can hardly be achieved."[86] The only way to ensure this is to comply with Security Council Resolutions 1325 and 1889 and to make sure that there are a number of women in all delegations.

That point was also made about Kosovo by Lesley Abdela, who served as part of the UN Mission in Kosovo in 1999: "Despite an absolute immensity of warnings signaling that the overwhelmingly men-dominated international missions were getting things wrong, the women of Bosnia and Kosovo remained excluded from any concrete involvement in negotiations, post-conflict reconstruction planning, and even from the democratization process itself." Abdela then reflects on how women were excluded from the senior decision-making positions, which, "combined with the very damaging gender ignorance/blindness of the senior men posted to these missions, were key contributing factors to the chaotic and costly mess that ensued in the civilian reconstruction process."[87]

After the Conflict Ends: Post-Conflict Reconstruction

It is clear that there is a process in which planning for peace starts during the conflict. Here, too, women's voices and input about the construction or reconstruction of the society after the conflict ends are essential. As the Expert Group Meeting noted, "Women have a broader view of conflict resolution, and this may positively affect the resolution of the conflict. Women may often see what male decision-makers fail to see, especially the effect of various kinds of resolution on the ground, and especially their effect on women."[88] In most cases, when women look to the construction or reconstruction of society following the conflict (something that they think about during the conflict), they generally see the need to consider more than just the end of violence; they also want to address the underlying social, cultural, economic, and political issues that contributed to the outbreak of the conflict. Further, some of the needs of the society following a conflict are unique to women or are especially relevant for women, including trauma counseling for rape victims and victims of domestic violence, resettlement of refugees, and establishment of property rights and custody rights.[89]

This point is echoed in case after case where women were engaged in peace or conflict-resolution negotiations. That is, that women approach such negotiations from a "big picture" perspective in which resolving a conflict is more than about simply ending violence, but it involves reconstructing a future where such violence is less likely.

For example, Chris Corrin offers the specific example of weaknesses in the creation of the new Criminal Code in Kosova[90] in 2000 as part of the reconstruction of the society after the 1999 NATO bombing to show the importance of sensitivity to "women's issues." As she points out, that region was being reconstructed following the war, "a new Criminal Code was under review, with key priorities of sexual violence, domestic violence and juvenile justice." She notes how the "lack of a fully functioning legal system has gender implications as judges with no gender awareness have extensive powers of judgment and decision-making, often much to the disadvantage of women." She cites specific examples showing that "women seldom receive a favorable court decision in support of their right to custody of children" and "women's rights to property is not generally recognized and, in cases of violence against women or children (including incest), the courts tend to free the husband and/or father on grounds of 'lack of evidence' despite the presentation of photos and witness statements in evidence."[91]

Corrin's points are also reflected in a report from a seminar on women and peacebuilding in Africa that notes that "at the national level, post-conflict negotiations often provide a unique window of opportunity for ensuring increased political representation of women and to demand equality under the law." The report then lists some of the women in Africa who have managed to attain high decision-making positions: Ellen Johnson-Sirleaf, as president of Liberia; women in vice presidential positions in South Africa, Zimbabwe, and Burundi; and women who serve as prime ministers in Mozambique and Sao Tome and Principe. While these women are unique for their achievements, the report also notes that "women are also finding ways to be heard at community and local decision-making processes," which is far less unique and far more consistent with the dominant patterns of women's political activism.[92] As these examples show, if the post-conflict society is to change in its rebuilding, then women's voices need to be heard.

It is critically important to have women's voices represented not only at the table negotiating the end of conflict, but in determining what the post-conflict society should look like. Furthermore, injecting women's voices not only assures that their needs will be met, but also that underlying social issues that might have contributed to the outbreak of the conflict will be addressed. Thus, the negotiations are not only conflict-resolution issues, but they are also potentially ways to avoid future conflicts. Again quoting Corrin, "Given that many military conflicts are often continuations of previous wars, the roots of these conflicts require analysis and civic groups, especially feminist groups, need to be involved in such inquiries given their expertise and political will to talk across differences toward agreement."[93]

This suggests that women's voices must be heard if the reconstruction process is to succeed and the society to remain not only conflict free, but responsive to the needs of *all* members of the society. Increasing attention has been given to the contributions that women can make not only to conflict resolution, but also to the reconstruction efforts that follow.

There is often a correlation among women's involvement in the struggle, their ability to get a seat at the table, and their role in helping to define the post-conflict world. For example, "The visibility of women in campaigns and in post-apartheid policy-making debates in South Africa is sufficient evidence that women's involvement in the struggle against apartheid was not minor. South African women's role in their own organization, and as fellow activists in the liberation movement, is well documented. Yet when negotiations began, women had to *campaign* for inclusion" (emphasis in original). One activist interviewed noted that "the inclusion of women at the negotiation table did not come naturally; former women activists played a fundamental role in ensuring not only the inclusion of women at the negotiation table, but also the inclusion of gender issues in the constitution of South Africa."[94]

In South Africa women played a significant role in the establishment and structure of the Truth and Reconciliation Commission (TRC), which is now "held as an example of a transitional justice mechanism that was able to both establish a more complete or 'truthful' historic record of the apartheid era and contribute to the healing of a nation and the reconciliation of former enemies, both individual and institutional." Among the critical contributions that women activists made was "in encouraging the TRC to take cognizance of the constraints that initially framed its work, and called for a gender-sensitive TRC, which led to special hearings focusing on women's experiences during apartheid." The presence and awareness of these women also ensured that the structure of the TRC would not replicate the patriarchal structure of the society. And, given the fact that "women experience conflict in a particular way, their contributions to the TRC, as witnesses, commissioners, and personnel, are important to understanding South Africa's transition to a democracy." The in-depth study of women's contributions to the TRC is careful to note that it "does not assert that women are naturally more peace-loving than men; neither does this study assume that all women share a common experience of conflict and of transitional justice processes." Rather, it acknowledges that in order to understand South Africa's transition from apartheid to democracy, it is necessary to understand women's contributions.[95]

Barriers to Women's Political Involvement

It is important to note the barriers that work *against* women's involvement in political life, although when we talk about women's political activism, it means that at least some women have found a way to overcome or to work within the existing social and political barriers. There are a number of such barriers to women's political activism that can quickly and easily be identified, not least of which are the structural ones that perpetuate a male-dominated, patriarchal political system that has little room for women. This is a difficult one for women to address, although clearly some women have been very successful at doing so. But there are a number of other barriers as well that, when taken as a whole, mitigate against women's direct involvement. On the other hand, when women find a way to address them, they can be very effective political actors.

In some cases these barriers to women's involvement are overt, such as prohibiting or limiting women's access to the vote or even running for office.[96] But in other cases they are far more covert and insidious and stem from the patriarchal structure of the political system that perpetuates a set of stereotypical values and attitudes that exclude women while technically granting them the right to vote or gain access to the political system.[97] Women may also face physical threats from local men as well as the police forces within a society if they attempt to participate in the political process.[98] As a result, in many cases the most effective way for women to engage is to do so using more traditional roles, for example, as wives and mothers, and often indirectly by working with NGOs or other groups not officially associated with the government. This not only provides the women with a comfort zone within which they can operate, but it also allows them to be accepted rather than to be seen as threatening. However, as noted in an earlier chapter, this also runs the risk of minimizing or diminishing the role they play, or essentializing women.

The Northern Ireland Voluntary Trust report, noted earlier in the chapter, addressed the issue of women's under-representation in political life in Northern Ireland and identified four barriers to women's active involvement in the political system that can be generalized across a number of countries: attitudinal, political culture, educational, and practical. This is not to suggest that if each or all barriers were removed that women would be more active or engaged. However, the point is that these barriers work to prevent women's involvement, and they must be overcome.

The range of barriers that the trust identified (and which many scholars also point out) is interesting not only for the ones that are included, but for the ways in which they affect women much more so than men. For example, attitudinal barriers are seen as "the lack of appropriate and inspiring role models for women," which is clearly not a factor that affects men.[99] As Hunt and Posa assert, fighting wars is considered to be the male domain, and thus any peace should also be within the purview of men. Such gendered attitudes preclude women's participation.[100] The second barrier is the prevailing culture of the local political system and processes that "are considered to militate against women's involvement."[101] Complementing this is the next barrier, which is educational, specifically, "the lack of basic political education, which would serve to increase knowledge and understanding of structure and processes, and encourage people to question more critically."[102] Clearly, if women are not educated about or aware of the structure and processes of politics, they are not in any position to know how to confront or to work within the dominant political culture. The fourth and final barrier that this group identified is the practical, or the lack of resources available for women.[103] Women's organizations need funding and training in management skills, as well as being trained to lobby.[104] This led to the conclusion that "sexism in general, coupled with the public perception of women's role, and of individual women politicians, reinforce many of the barriers outlined."[105]

A different, but related, practical barrier to women's participation was noted by Norma Shearer of the Training for Women Network at a conference on women and peace, that is, that part of the reason women were and are constrained in what they can do is limited access to child care. Until that basic need can be addressed, she claims, women's access will always be limited.[106] Again, this issue generally is not a factor for men.

These barriers can and have been overcome by individual women, but the difficulty in doing so was noted by women who were successful in breaking into the political system and who recognized what they had to overcome to do so.

While acknowledging the devastating effects of these barriers to political involvement on many women, the report of the trust also provides a positive recommendation about how these barriers can be addressed, if not overcome: Women are "disheartened by mainstream politics" and feel that they can do little to change it. Therefore, it is necessary to begin to address the current culture, style, and sexism *at a community level* by encouraging women to consider "what it is they can do locally." "It was recognized by many of the women interviewed that there is still quite a gap between activism at the local level and in the wider public sphere. Therefore . . . there is a need to make provision for progression routes from the community level to the wider public sphere, for women who chose to work at that level (emphasis added)."[107] As many feminist organizations can attest, the long-term goal of changing entrenched gendered power structures is important in order to enable women to participate fully in the public sphere.

Patricia Lawsley is the Northern Ireland Commissioner for Children and Young People and an elected representative to the Northern Ireland Assembly from the Social and Democratic Labor Party, one of the Catholic/Republican parties. In an interview in 2007, she noted that breaking into the political structure was difficult for her, and for women in general. She had five children at home, and she supported the work of her husband, a politician. Because of her political ties through her husband, she was eventually asked to stand for election, which she did. She won. But, as she also noted, this had an impact on her family life. In addition, it is "not cheap to be a politician," and she was always conscious of the need to keep finding funding so that she could run for office.

In the interview, Ms. Lawsley mentioned that she herself was from a working-class background with no higher education. She said that, like other women, initially she was unaware of what she could bring to the process, and she now makes it a point to mentor other women. But, she commented, it took her about fourteen years to "grow into her position" and to take advantage of life experiences, which is what she brings to her current position. The perspective that Ms. Lawsley identifies and the set of experiences that she brings to the political system are not unique to her but are common across a range of women.

Interview with Patricia Lawsley at her office, Belfast, Northern Ireland, November 19, 2007.

Conclusion:
Women, Activism, and Social Justice Issues

It is clear that women bring to the peace table an agenda that is far larger than resolving a conflict or ending the violence, although these important goals cannot be minimized. Women who engage in conflict-resolution/peace negotiations seem to be interested in understanding the issues that led the society into conflict initially (issues of structural violence) so that they can be addressed and corrected in the belief that this will help avoid future conflict. Generally this broad range of issues falls under the general categories of human rights and social justice, specifically, the desire to create a society characterized by a respect for human rights and the rights of all individuals. But, as we noted in an earlier work, this does not suggest "that women are more 'peace-like' and less conflictual than men. Rather, what we conclude from our research is that women seem to approach questions of peace and conflict *differently* from men, no doubt to a large extent because of the fact that they are seeing the impact of those conflicts from a different perspective" (emphasis added).[108]

Although having women participate in peace negotiations does not guarantee that gender equality or other "women's issues" will be addressed, their absence will usually assure that such issues will not be raised. Studies have shown that "in addition to placing gender issues more frequently on the peace agenda than men, women often introduce other conflict experiences and set different priorities for peacebuilding and rehabilitation. They tend to be the sole voices speaking out for women's rights and concerns . . . [and] as the primary caretakers, women tend to prioritize education, health, nutrition, childcare, and human welfare needs." And "women's participation in peace talks can also widen the popular mandate for peace and lead to concrete measures."[109]

The literature supports the inclusive nature with which women tend to approach the negotiations.[110] Anderlini notes that the different perspective that women bring to the peace table "often leads women to advocate practical solutions in the building of peace." In fact, she continues, "women often reported that men and women frequently understand the purposes of peace talks differently, and come to the table with different motivations." Anderlini references Cheryl Carolus, previously South Africa's high commissioner to Great Britain and a woman who was actively involved with the negotiations in that country. In that case, "the women's coalition lobbied hard for measures that would make the new government open to constituencies that had traditionally been excluded from the political process." Quoting Carolus directly adds another dimension to what women bring to the table: "'It wasn't just a question of putting laws down on a piece of paper. It was about practical things, such as how the right to land would allow a female-headed household in a rural area to have a sustainable livelihood. *It was about being respectful of people's right to choose the life they want*" (emphasis added).[111]

The NIWC similarly defined its mission as far broader than getting a seat at the negotiating table—and in very practical terms. Even after the Good Friday Agreement was signed and ratified, the work of the coalition continued to stress the larger social issues seen in Northern Ireland. The report "Education for the Twenty-first Century," developed by the NIWC Education Policy Team, states clearly: "We in the Women's Coalition believe that our society must be built on acceptable and agreed core values. Our own core values are equality, human rights and inclusion." The report then goes on to stress the group's vision "of a peaceful, prosperous and well-educated society capable of meeting challenges of the twenty-first century with confidence and optimism."[112]

If women define their roles in seeking a peaceful and more just society far more broadly than simply the absence of conflict, it raises yet another important set of questions that UN Resolutions 1325 and 1889 were designed to address. Specifically, if women are interested in social justice issues and finding a way to resolve a conflict that would alter the structural issues that contributed to the onset of conflict in the first place, then why are women not included routinely in such negotiations and their ideas taken seriously? In other words, if women bring something important to the table, then why are they systematically excluded? Here, too, we must return to some of what was apparent from the start. Peace negotiations mirror the patriarchal structure of the political and social systems of the particular nation, which by their very nature exclude women. For example, the rise of nationalism that contributed to the onset of conflict only exacerbated that patriarchal structure, and often made women not only symbols, but also "prizes" of war. But, most important, women's political activism generally exists at the grassroots or community level, outside the formal political process. While this means they can often have the greatest impact in the areas that may be considered most important to them, almost of necessity it also means that they are excluded from more formal politics, that is, the area of national decision-making or, in this case, determining the future of the society. Thus, women political activists are often forced to make a choice: to work in the areas that they are most familiar and where they feel they can have the most immediate impact, or to try to break into the larger political decision-making structure and hope that their voices will be heard.

Notes

[1] The work in this section draws on some of the questions we tried to answer in Joyce P. Kaufman and Kristen P. Williams, "Conclusion," in *Women, the State, and War*, ed. Joyce P. Kaufman and Kristen P. Williams (Lanham, MD: Lexington, 2007). In that chapter we

drew on four cases to answer a range of questions about women's political activism, but also to raise a number of other questions. In this section we look at some of those questions, drawing upon a larger number of cases to help provide answers.

[2] Azza Karam, "Women in War and Peacebuilding," *International Feminist Journal of Politics* 3, no. 1 (April 2001): 12.

[3] Cynthia Cockburn, "The Continuum of Violence: A Gender Perspective on War and Peace," in *Sites of Violence: Gender and Conflict Zones*, ed. Wenona Giles and Jennifer Hyndman (Berkeley and Los Angeles: University of California Press, 2004), 44.

[4] Elaine Zuckerman and Marcia Greenberg, "The Gender Dimension of Post-Conflict Reconstruction: An Analytical Framework for Policymakers," *Gender and Development* 12, no. 3 (November 2004): 78.

[5] Kaufman and Williams, *Women, the State, and War*, 206.

[6] Swanee Hunt, "Moving beyond Silence: Women Waging Peace," *Listening to the Silences: Women and War*, ed. Helen Durham and Tracy Gurd (The Netherlands: Koninklijke Brill BV, 2005), 251. Swanee Hunt was US ambassador to Austria from 1993 to 1997.

[7] Elisabeth Porter, "The Challenge of Dialogue across Difference," in *Gender, Democracy, and Inclusion in Northern Ireland*, ed. Carmel Roulston and Celia Davis (New York: Palgrave, 2001).

[8] Donna Pankhurst, "Women, Gender, and Peacebuilding," Working Paper 5, University of Bradford (August 2000), 1. Available on the www.brad.ac.uk website.

[9] Tsjeard Bouta, Georg Frerks, and Ian Bannon, *Gender, Conflict, and Development* (Washington DC: The World Bank, 2004), 52.

[10] Karam, "Women in War and Peacebuilding," 14.

[11] Swanee Hunt and Cristina Posa, "Women Waging Peace," *Foreign Policy* 124 (May-June 2001): 41.

[12] V. Spike Peterson and Anne Sisson Runyan, *Global Gender Issues* (Boulder, CO: Westview Press, 1993), 179.

[13] Donna Pankhurst, "The 'Sex War' and Other Wars: Towards a Feminist Approach to Peace Building," *Development in Practice* 12, nos. 2/3 (May 2003): 161.

[14] "Workshop on Peace through Human Rights and Understanding," Navan, Ireland, October 12–17, 1986, Workshop summary, 13. Accessed at the Women's Library, London, June 2008.

[15] Inger Skjelsbaek, "Gendered Battlefields: A Gender Analysis of Peace and Conflict" (Oslo: International Peace Research Institute, October 1997), 11. Available on the www.prior.no website.

[16] Tami Amanda Jacoby, *Women in Zones of Conflict: Power and Resistance in Israel* (Quebec: McGill-Queen's University Press, 2005), 13.

[17] Peterson and Runyan, *Global Gender Issues*, 179.

[18] Christine Chinkin and Hilary Charlesworth, "Building Women into Peace: The International Legal Framework," *Third World Quarterly* 27, no. 5 (2006): 942.

[19] Elisabeth Porter, "Women, Political Decision-Making, and Peace-Building," *Global Change, Peace & Security* 15, 3 (October 2003): 250.

[20] J. Ann Tickner, *Gender in International Relations: Feminist Perspectives on Achieving Global Security* (New York: Columbia University Press, 1992), 59.

[21] See Kaufman and Williams, *Women, the State, and War.*

[22] Laura Sjoberg and Caron E. Gentry, *Mothers, Monsters, Whores: Women's Violence in Global Politics* (London: Zed Books, 2007), 4.

[23] Sumantra Bose, *Contested Lands: Israel-Palestine, Kashmir, Bosnia, Cyprus, and Sri Lanka* (Cambridge, MA: Harvard University Press, 2007), 38.

[24] Joshua S. Goldstein, *War and Gender: How Gender Shapes the War System and Vice Versa* (Cambridge: Cambridge University Press, 2001), 327.

[25] Elissa Helms, "Women as Agents of Ethnic Reconciliation? Women's NGOs and International Intervention in Postwar Bosnia-Herzegovina," *Women's Studies International Forum* 26, no. 1 (2003): 16.

[26] Shireen Hassim, *Women's Organizations and Democracy in South Africa: Contesting Authority* (Madison: University of Wisconsin Press, 2006), 81.

[27] Jacklyn Cock, *Women and War in South Africa* (Cleveland, OH: Pilgrim Press, 1993), 181.

[28] Helms, "Women as Agents of Ethnic Reconciliation?" 16, 21.

[29] Bose, *Contested Lands*, 49.

[30] United Nations Division for the Advancement of Women, and International Peace Research Institute (Oslo), Expert Group Meeting, Political Decision-Making and Conflict Resolution: The Impact of Gender Difference, Santo Domingo, Dominican Republic, October 1996, para. 58.

[31] Ibid., para. 64.

[32] Historically, the onset of the Troubles can be traced back to the early part of the twentieth century and the divisions within Ireland that were formalized by the Government of Ireland Act of 1920. For a short history, see Kaufman and Williams, *Women, the State, and War*, 159–64. That text includes references to other, more detailed histories of the onset of the troubles.

[33] For a detailed description of the NIWC from its creation through the negotiations, see Kate Fearon, *Women's Work: The Story of the Northern Ireland Women's Coalition* (Belfast: The Blackstaff Press Limited, 1999).

[34] "Report of the Northern Ireland Women's Coalition Meeting Held on Saturday 11th February 2006 in the Aisling Centre, Enniskillen," unpublished, accessed at the Linen Hall Library, archives of the NIWC, June 2008.

[35] Bouta, Frerks, and Bannon, *Gender, Conflict, and Development*, 52.

[36] Cynthia Cockburn, *From Where We Stand: War, Women's Activism and Feminist Analysis* (London: Zed Books, 2007), 141.

[37] Porter, "Women, Political Decision-Making, and Peace-Building," 245–46, 253.

[38] Margaret Ward, "Gender, Citizenship and the Future of the Northern Ireland Peace Process," paper provided by the author. The paper was subsequently published in *Irish Feminist Studies* 41, nos. 1/2 (Spring/Summer 2006): 262–83. For an interesting perspective on the efforts of women activists in Israel to incorporate women's participation in decision-making in Israeli law as elucidated in Resolution 1325, see Paula Mills, "Working to Promote 1325 in Israel: Opportunities and Challenges Facing Activist Women and Isha L'Isha," Working Paper, The Boston Consortium on Gender, Security, and Human Rights (November 29, 2006). She notes that during the Oslo peace process, women did not serve

on any committees or teams, but they were behind the scenes. She writes, "They are in the offices and writing all of the contracts, they are the lawyers writing and preparing all the papers that are then brought to the negotiating teams (which are a hundred percent men on both sides—Palestinian men and Israeli men). The men are sitting and doing the negotiations with contracts and papers that have been written by women—who are invisible" (7).

[39] "No Standing, Few Prospects: How Peace Is Failing South Sudanese Female Combatants and WAAFG [Women Associated with Armed Forces and Groups]" *Sudan Issue Brief,* Small Arms Survey 13 (September 2008): 1, 4.

[40] Porter, "Women, Political Decision-Making, and Peace-Building," 254–56.

[41] Ibid., 254–55.

[42] United Nations, "Security Council Demands Immediate and Complete Halt to Acts of Sexual Violence Against Civilians in Conflict Zones, Unanimously Adopting Resolution 1820 (2008)," UN Department of Public Information SC/9364 (June 19, 2008). Available on the www.un.org website.

[43] United Nations, "Resolution 1888 (2009)," United Nations Security Council S/RES/ 1888 (September 30, 2009).

[44] United Nations, "Resolution 1889 (2009)," United Nations Security Council S/RES/ 1889 (October 5, 2009). Available on the daccess-dds-ny.un.org website.

[45] Anderlini notes that in 2006, "there were no women in the multiparty Nepali peace negotiations. In Uganda . . . the opposition group, the Lord's Resistance Army (LRA), had a single woman on its team, but the government had none. Women remain absent as third-party mediators and even as representatives of the UN Secretary-General in most conflict-affected countries." Sanam Naraghi Anderlini, *Women Building Peace: What They Do, Why It Matters* (Boulder, CO: Lynne Rienner, 2007), 54.

[46] Porter, "Women, Political Decision-Making, and Peace-Building," 255.

[47] Anderlini, *Women Building Peace,* 58.

[48] Porter, "Women, Political Decision-Making, and Peace-Building," 251.

[49] Kvinna till Kvinna, *Engendering the Peace Process: A Gender Approach to Dayton and Beyond* (Stockholm: The Kvinna till Kvinna Foundation, 2000), 9.

[50] Hunt, "Moving beyond Silence," 252.

[51] Sanam Naraghi Anderlini, "Women at the Peace Table: Making a Difference" (New York: United Nations Fund for Women, 2000), 34.

[52] Hanan Ashwari, quoted in ibid., 35.

[53] Records of the International Alliance of Women, 1904–1991, archived August 2005, 1, accessed at the Women's Library, London, June 2008.

[54] Ibid.

[55] Goldstein, *War and Gender,* 324.

[56] Ibid., 325.

[57] Louise O'Meara, "Additional Measures Required to Address the Issue of the Under-represented Women in Political Life," unpublished report prepared by the Northern Ireland Voluntary Trust, December 1997, 12, accessed at the Linen Hall Library, Belfast, June 2008.

[58] Bouta, Frerks, and Bannon, *Gender, Conflict, and Development,* 73.

[59] Expert Group Meeting, Political Decision-Making and Conflict Resolution, para. 65, (a) and (c).

[60] Elisabeth Porter, "Identity, Location, Plurality: Women, Nationalism, and Northern Ireland," in *Women, Ethnicity, and Nationalism: The Politics of Transition*, ed. Rick Wilford and Robert L. Miller (London: Routledge, 1998), 50.

[61] Monica McWilliams, "Struggling for Peace and Justice: Reflections on Women's Activism in Northern Ireland," *Journal of Women's History* 6/7, nos. 4/1 (Winter/Spring 1995): 18.

[62] Porter, "Identity, Location, Plurality," 48.

[63] Hassim, *Women's Organizations and Democracy in South Africa*, 27, 256.

[64] Isabel Coral Cordero, "Social Organizations: From Victims to Actors in Peace Building," in *Victims, Perpetrators, or Actors? Gender, Armed Conflict, and Political Violence*, ed. Caroline O. N. Moser and Fiona C. Clark (London: Zed Books, 2001), 161.

[65] It is important to note that many of these grassroots organizations are not exclusively made up of women. In fact, there are many organizations working for peace that include men as well as women. However, in many cases they are identified with women or are perceived to have feminine characteristics. For example, the Israeli group Parents Against Silence, formed as a direct response to the Israeli war against Lebanon in 1982, was quickly dubbed Mothers against Silence "because of its disproportionately female composition and its feminine discourse that emphasized the private sphere and a mother's concern for her child" (Jacoby, *Women in Zones of Conflict*, 72).

[66] Anderlini, *Women Building Peace*, 66.

[67] Kaufman and Williams, *Women, the State, and War*, 144.

[68] The notes from these seminars were accessed at the Women's Library Reading Room in London, England, in June 2008 by Joyce Kaufman. She is very grateful to the staff for its help.

[69] Jane S. Jaquette, "Women and Democracy: Regional Differences and Contrasting Views," *Journal of Democracy* 12, no. 3 (July 2001): 114–15.

[70] Pankhurst, "The 'Sex War' and Other Wars," 168.

[71] Anderlini, *Women Building Peace*, 59.

[72] Bouta, Frerks, and Bannon, *Gender, Conflict, and Development*, 53.

[73] Anderlini, *Women Building Peace*, 42.

[74] Anderlini, *Women Building Peace*, 43.

[75] In Kaufman's conversation with Margaret Ward on November 20, 2007, in Belfast, Ward made the point that women in South Africa made a conscious decision to work with women in Northern Ireland in order to help the peace process. As a result, there are strong links between the two countries.

[76] Anderlini, *Women Building Peace*, 43.

[77] Ibid., 44.

[78] For a detailed study of the NIWC, see Fearon, *Women's Work*.

[79] (Baroness) May Blood, *Watch My Lips, I'm Speaking* (Dublin: Gill and Macmillan, 2007), 151–52.

[80] Fearon, *Women's Work*, 158.

[81] Blood, *Watch My Lips*, 154.

[82] Ibid., 153–54.

[83] The authors are very grateful to Bronagh Hinds for her insights and recollections about the NIWC, its history, and its impact. Joyce Kaufman met with Ms. Hinds in Belfast on November 20, 2007. Hinds is currently a senior research fellow at the Institute of Governance, Queens University, Belfast.

[84] The authors attempted to get an interview with or responses from Richard Holbrooke, the chief architect of the Dayton Agreement, about the process and the role (or absence) of women, but he never responded to their inquiry.

[85] Kvinna till Kvinna, *Engendering the Peace Process*, 10.

[86] Kvinna till Kvinna, *Engendering the Peace Process*, 10.

[87] Lesley Abdela, "Kosovo: Missed Opportunities, Lessons for the Future," in *Development, Women and War: Feminist Perspectives,* ed. Haleh Afshar and Deborah Eade (Oxford, England: OXFAM GB, 2004), 89–90.

[88] Expert Group Meeting, Political Decision-Making and Conflict Resolution, para. 51.

[89] Maja Korac, "Gender, Conflict, and Peace-Building: Lessons from the Conflict in the Former Yugoslavia," *Women's International Studies Forum* 29 (2006): 514–16; Chris Corrin, "Post-Conflict Reconstruction and Gender Analysis in Kosova," *International Feminist Journal of Politics* 3, no. 1 (April 2000): 83–84. Corrin also notes an issue facing women and girls in Kosovo in the post-conflict stage, namely, access to education. Girls face barriers to accessing schooling, including poverty (families are more willing to fund their boys' education), age ("reflecting fear that girls in their late teens will be too old to find marriage partners"), and security ("fear of being physically attacked or raped"). When girls have limited access to education, the long-term consequences are lack of economic opportunities and further miring of girls/women in poverty (Corrin, "Post-Conflict Reconstruction and Gender Analysis in Kosova," 90).

[90] Corrin uses the "the spelling Kosova (rather than Kosovo) as this is how the majority Kosovar Albanian population names the country. Kosovo is used in sections of the international community and is acceptable to the Serbian regime" (Corrin, "Post-Conflict Reconstruction and Gender Analysis in Kosova," 96n2.

[91] Ibid., 84.

[92] "Women in Peacebuilding in Africa," seminar report, October 27 and 28, 2005.

[93] Corrin, "Post-Conflict Reconstruction and Gender Analysis in Kosova," 79.

[94] Pumla Gobodo-Madikizela, "Women's Contributions to South Africa's Truth and Reconciliation Commission," Women Waging Peace Policy Commission, February 2005, 7.

[95] Ibid., 17, 3.

[96] In 2005, Kuwait's parliament granted full political rights to women, thereby allowing them to vote or run for office. This required an amendment to Kuwait's elections law that removed the word "men" from Article 1. (Hassan M. Fattah, "Kuwait Grants Political Rights to Its Women," *The New York Times*, May 17, 2005.) Saudi Arabia still does not allow women to vote or to participate in elections.

[97] Porter, "Women, Political Decision-Making, and Peace-Building," 248.

[98] Pankhurst, "The 'Sex War' and Other Wars," 163.

[99] O'Meara, "Additional Measures Required to Address the Issue of the Under-represented Women in Political Life," 4.

[100] Hunt and Posa, "Women Waging Peace," 46.

[101] O'Meara, "Additional Measures Required to Address the Issue of the Under-represented Women in Political Life," 4.

[102] Ibid., 5.

[103] Ibid., 7.

[104] Pankhurst, "The 'Sex War' and Other Wars," 163.

[105] O'Meara, "Additional Measures Required to Address the Issue of the Under-represented Women in Political Life," 7.

[106] Norma Shearer (chief executive officer, Training for Women Network), "A Helping Hand," talk given at Peace by Piece, International Women's Conference, June 24–26, 2008, Belfast, Northern Ireland.

[107] O'Meara, "Additional Measures Required to Address the Issue of the Under-represented Women in Political Life," 7.

[108] Kaufman and Williams, *Women, the State, and War*, 207.

[109] Bouta, Frerks, and Bannon, *Gender, Conflict, and Development*, 52.

[110] See, for example, Fearon, *Women's Work*.

[111] Anderlini, *Women at the Peace Table*, 33.

[112] NIWC, Education Policy Team, "Education for the Twenty-first Century: The Report of the Post-Primary Review Body" (June 2002), 1. Unpublished report, accessed at the Linen Hall Library, Belfast, Northern Ireland, NIWC archives, June 2008.

Chapter 6

Where Are the Women?

Answering the Question: Where Are the Women?

One of the enduring questions of international relations revolves around the issue of peace and war. States and groups within states continue to engage in violent behavior toward other states and groups. In the traditional IR field, scholars grapple with understanding the causes of war and peace. Yet, given the patriarchal structure of most states and societies, it is interesting to note that most scholars do not ask questions about the impact of war and peace on women. Feminist IR scholars seek to rectify that omission by pointedly asking: where are the women? What one finds is that women are there—especially during and after conflict. Some women become politically active, seeking to stop conflicts before they begin or escalate, or trying to end conflicts once they have begun. Some women join the fight as combatants, either for the government's military or rebel forces. Other women flee as internally displaced peoples within their own countries or as refugees in other countries. In all these scenarios, war affects women. War affects women when they are no longer secure in their homes, when they no longer can access food for their families, when they can no longer earn a living, when they no longer have access to healthcare, and when they can no longer protect themselves from men's sexual violence.

Recognizing that women are affected by war and conflict, particularly intrastate or internal wars and conflicts, we set out to ask and, it is hoped, answer several questions regarding the ways in which women respond to situations of conflict and war—before, during, and after. We asked about women's political activism, namely, why and how women decide to take political action, what actions they take, and how they have an impact on conflict, given that it is men who overwhelmingly make the decision to go to war and to negotiate the peace. While we recognize that some women choose to engage in war and conflict, either in traditional supportive roles (as nurses, as mothers and wives encouraging their sons and husbands to fight) or more directly in terms of actual fighting (as combatants or arms smugglers), we focused here on women who chose to work for peace. The central question of the book has been: what happened to the women? In unpacking this question, we asked: What happened to the women when society was moving toward conflict and war? What happened to the women when war and conflict had begun and continued? What happened to the women when the war or conflict moved toward its end and the process of rebuilding and reconciliation began? Were women at the negotiating table? If so, did they make a difference in the kind of peace that was made? Did they make a difference in the post-conflict peacebuilding when society emerged from war? Specifically, what happened to the women who were active politically in promoting peace and an end to conflict when the conflict finally ended?

In this concluding chapter we revisit the main themes of the book, discuss some general conclusions, and provide suggestions for future research.

The Onset and Outbreak of War and Conflict: The Impact on Women

We found that as a state or society moves toward war, the signs become clearer that changes are in the offing. A government begins to prepare for war rather than maintain peace (guns versus butter). Government expenditures for war materials increase, while expenditures for social services (education, healthcare) decrease. As Cynthia Cockburn asserts, the decrease in expenditures on public services are more costly for women and children, costs that occur before the actual war or conflict erupts.[1] Understanding security as more than just state security, in traditional IR parlance, but also as security for women more broadly defined (economic, social, physical) enables us to see how conflict and war threaten the security of women. Awareness that as a state moves toward war women's security is threatened is necessary for understanding women's reactions and responses.

When conflict does erupt, women are affected. This is not to say, of course, that men are not affected by conflict; they are. However, as Chapter 3 showed, the impact of conflict on women is in many ways different, particularly given that most women in society are civilians rather than combatants, and they experience gender-based violence in ways that men do not. Women experience domestic violence by their husbands as well as sexual violence and rape at the hands of soldiers. Such gender-based violence reinforces the domination of men over women in general, and one group of men over another, particularly in the case of ethnic/nationalist conflicts. Forced impregnation is an insidious aspect of gender-based violence, furthering the idea of domination of one group over another. The humiliation women experience from the rape itself as well as the birth of a child of the enemy distorts the idea of motherhood as a symbolic marker of ethnicity and national identity. Gender-based violence is targeted at a woman as an individual as well as at the ethnic/national group as a whole. Even with the international community's recent efforts to address the issue of gender-based violence (such as the International

Criminal Court, international tribunals, and UN Security Council Resolutions), women continue to experience this violence, particularly in times of conflict, as illustrated by the continuing conflicts in Darfur, Sudan, and the Democratic Republic of the Congo.

In addition to gender-based violence, wars and conflict leave large numbers of people displaced. According to the UNHCR website, at least half of the world's refugees are women. Women refugees face many challenges, including sexual attack, lack of access to effective and adequate healthcare, lack of employment, and difficulty obtaining shelter and food. These challenges are, in essence, security issues for women and their families. The international community has taken measures to deal with refugees, particularly through the work of the UNHCR. While UNHCR plays an important role in addressing the needs of refugees, its policies often reinforce essentialist understandings of women and gender, where women's participation in decision-making, in the case of Bosnia, for example, is "on the basis of their continued ties to the home and the (patriarchal) family," according to Elissa Helms.[2]

Women have responded to these situations (sexual violence and rape; displacement) in times of war and conflict by becoming politically active. For example, women activists have pushed governments to support the UN Security Council Resolutions that focus specifically on gender-based violence during conflict. In choosing to become politically active, women gain agency.

Women's Political Activism in War and Conflict

When the war or conflict begins, some women will become politically active to end the war. We have sought to demonstrate how women, who are traditionally excluded from the decision about whether to go to war and then from the decisions about the conduct of the war itself, move from the private to the public sphere, taking a more active role either in the informal structures or formal structures. Given that the decision-making, particularly at the national level, is usually done by men, within a patriarchal political and social structure, women's political peace activism tends to occur within their own communities, at the local or grassroots level, as we show in Chapters 4 and 5. Women's exclusion from the formal political system leads many women to come together to address and meet needs (housing, childcare, healthcare, and so forth) in times of war, in which they are essentially unified by shared experience. Many women do not self-identify as political, yet their actions and activism can be defined as political. Moving from the private to the public sphere is, in fact, a political act. In doing so, women's influence on the political process is possible.

For those women peace activists who do self-identify their activism as political, much of their work is moving beyond the immediate needs of ending the conflict to broader, long-term structural changes. Recognizing that the formal political power structure is gendered (subordinating women to men), some women are empowered to seek to change the structure. Many attempt to do so through the formal political structure, while others do so through informal processes. Either way, these women demand a change in the existing gendered power structure of the state and society. Achieving that goal is difficult as long as entrenched power structures continue to elevate men's power and position in society above women's. While that goal is more often than not difficult to achieve, conflict and war sometimes provides an opening for women to enter the political process.

Women in Post-Conflict Peacemaking and Peacebuilding

Given the important role that women can and have played at peace negotiations and the existence of formal international resolutions encouraging if not requiring the presence of women, then where are the women? Why are there not more women who actively participate in peace negotiations? And what happens to these women after the conflict ends?

According to Bouta, Frerks, and Bannon, "While women are often active in the informal peace processes, they are largely absent from formal peace processes." The authors continue to say that the "UN argues that women need to be included in formal peace processes to build greater post-conflict gender balance and a more inclusive peace. Women's participation in the peace process and mainstreaming their involvement into the peace accords lay the groundwork for engendering post-conflict reconstruction and rehabilitation." Despite these advantages, and there are numerous examples that indicate that women's participation in conflict resolution, peace negotiations, and discussions about reconciliation and restructuring society have been beneficial, Bouta, Frerks, and Bannon also state the obvious when they write that "most political institutions tend to exclude women." Hence, rather than working within the formal political structure, when they are involved many women choose to work outside that structure. Thus, "it is not surprising that, compared to men, relatively few women become involved in formal peace processes, from negotiations that often begin in the midst of conflict and continue through the various phases of the transition to peace. These processes tend to remain male-dominated; women are underrepresented at all levels, in negotiating teams representing the warring parties, and in other institutions invited to the negotiation table."[3]

If women's participation can have such a positive impact both on the negotiation and the post-conflict social structure, and if international organizations such as the United Nations advocate for the greater inclusion of women, where are they? Why are women not more involved with negotiations or a greater presence at the negotiating table?

Part of the reason is structural, as asserted in Chapter 5. Since negotiations to end a conflict have as their primary actors political and often military leaders, and since women are generally absent from such positions, then it follows that women would not have a presence at the negotiating table. Therefore, women have either to create structures that will give them a place at the table, as was the case with NIWC, or work outside the formal process through the creation of or work with existing NGOs, political parties, or lobbying groups that advocate for a similar position. And even in those cases where women do manage to play a role during the conflict or in the peace negotiations, these do not translate into a place for them in the post-conflict political or decision-making structures.

Also noted in Chapter 5, one of the reasons is that women are not trained to— nor do they know how to—overcome the barriers or obstacles that hinder their involvement. Their lack of education and training means that they do not know how to or have the confidence to break the male-dominated barriers that guard the peace negotiation process. As we have also seen, their lack of involvement is not because of lack of interest or commitment. Women are involved in working for peace, although often at the community level, and it has proven to be inordinately difficult to jump from that level to the national or international level at which most peace negotiations take place. But it is not impossible, and there are examples of women and women's groups doing so.

Furthermore, building support at the grassroots level can often be a way to put pressure on the politicians and decision-makers, eventually resulting in change. The NIWC, after it could not get any candidates elected to the Assembly in the 2003 elections, put forward a number of options for the party: remain as a political party, become a political lobbying group, become a women's movement NGO, or disband. These options were discussed at the February 11, 2006, meeting of the coalition. The group started by reflecting on what its initial goals were, including creating "a space for women's voices at the talks" and raising "the profile of women, interests of women at a formal political level." In addition to achieving these goals, the group acknowledged that it had accomplished a great deal more, including making other parties "take women seriously and stand them in electable seats," providing a "training ground for women to go into political activity, public life, policy work, etc.," and changing the face of politics, "the mode of operations/the language of discourse." The members also acknowledged the amount of work that still needed to be done, including convincing the government and the public "of particular value of women's engagement in political/public life" and recognizing the need for more women in political and public life. Nonetheless, the group voted to disband the party.[4] While some of the women, like Monica McWilliams and Patricia Lawsley, remained involved in the political system by serving on commissions, others went back to doing "what we do best," that is "trying to change society from the bottom up," in the words of Jane Morrice, former NIWC member to the Northern Ireland Assembly from Northdown. Ms. Morrice also noted that even though the NIWC had disbanded, women needed to "keep pushing for a space at the top."[5]

A regional seminar sponsored by the International Alliance of Women was held in Colombo, Sri Lanka, in November 1975, three years after that country won its independence and approximately seven years before civil war broke out. The following was written in the record of the conference: "Since peace is vital to the whole human race, socio-economic development is important. Women form half the world's population and therefore their potential contribution should be directed to this end by being included in *all* decision-making bodies concerned with international peace and understanding."

International Alliance of Women, Records of the Southeast Regional Seminar, Colombo, Sri Lanka (November 6–11, 1975), 11, accessed at the Women's Library, London, June 2008.

If peace is to succeed and be sustained, women must be involved in the process of building it. And since it is highly unlikely that the existing patriarchal structures that diminish, minimize, or do not recognize the role that women can and do play will be disbanded or change, then it is incumbent upon women to learn how to work within, as well as to challenge the system. Only by doing so will women's voices truly be heard.

General Conclusions

In considering general conclusions for this book, we reflect on three elements: feminist versus traditional "motherist" activism; essentialist versus social constructivist approaches; and women as victims and agents. At the heart of each of these elements is an understanding of women's identities (whether self-defined or other-defined). Women (and men) have multiple identities, including national, ethnic, class, race, and gender identities. These identities are salient at different times, depending on circumstances. We were interested in exploring women's national and gender identities, as these identities are often fraught with tension in times of conflict. In times of nationalist/ethnic wars, women's ethnic or national identity may be perceived as more important than gender identity. Women, then, have a difficult time crossing ethnic/national lines and acting politically as women as a group. If there are women's identities that transcend ethnic/national identities, perhaps "women's issues" (as discussed in Chapter 2) can be addressed effectively, as evidenced by the cases of women's groups in Bosnia and Northern Ireland. Thus, an interesting question to consider is whether in times of war and conflict certain identities are more salient than other identities. If so, how does the salience of those identities affect women's ability to become politically active for peace? How does the salience of those identities affect women's ability to have a place at the peace negotiations and for the post-conflict peace-building?

For many women, their identity as women is found in their roles as mothers and wives. Those identities and perceived roles are important to understand women's political activism and women's movements. As Chapter 2 noted, not all women's movements are feminist movements. Many women's movements are explicitly not feminist movements, and, in fact, reject that categorization. Such women's movements, while very much about gender identity, address "women's issues," but do not seek to alter the patriarchal structure of society. Feminist movements call for an end to the existing gendered power structures and power relations in which men are dominant and women are subordinate, ensuring equality for both sexes/genders.

In times of war and conflict, states and ethnic/nationalist groups will utilize gendered imagery of women as wives and mothers in service of the state's or group's political goals. As is repeatedly shown in many cases, gender and nationalism converge so that fighting for the "mother country" or promoting ideas of women as peacemakers becomes the norm. When the conflict ends, women are expected to return to the private sphere, the home, reinforcing the traditional/essentialist gender identities, roles, and imagery. The challenge for feminist movements in times of conflict and war is to overcome those socially constructed gender identities in order to upend the patriarchal society and government that constrains women's ability to play an active role in decision-making as a society moves toward war and returns to peace. As long as women's gender identities are situated such that they are excluded explicitly or implicitly from formal politics, long-term structural changes are unlikely. The international community and individual states can promote the idea of the elevation of women at the peace talks and post-conflict rebuilding of society, but until concrete steps are taken—and women are actually a part of those conversations and decisions—patriarchal power structures will remain and endure.

Finally, what also stands out in examining women's peace activism is the issue of women as victims or agents. As we have demonstrated throughout this book, women are victims. Before a conflict begins, women become victims when the government or ethnic/nationalist groups invest in war preparation at the expense of healthcare and education. Women are victims when they experience sexual violence and violence by government and/or militia forces, or when they experience domestic violence in the home. Women are victims when they are forced to flee their homes, living in refugee camps, most often as heads of household, with little access to jobs, healthcare, and food. Women are victims when a conflict ends and they cannot return to their homes, are widowed, have no legal documents for asylum, or have no access to land.

Yet, whether participating in feminist movements or women's movements that are not explicitly feminist, women do have agency. The previous chapters have demonstrated that women become agents when they participate in informal and formal politics. Women have agency when they form grassroots organizations to secure food, healthcare, housing, and so forth for their communities, their families, and themselves. Women have agency when they demand a seat at the negotiating table. And women have agency when they demand that states adhere to UN Security Council resolutions that make sexual violence and rape war crimes, and resolutions that demand that women have a decision-making role as societies move toward peace and reconciliation.

Recognizing that women are both victims and agents, even within patriarchal structures, necessitates that we study the impact of war and conflict on women. Asking the questions of what happens to them and where they are matters for a more comprehensive understanding of war and conflict. We hope that we have contributed to the existing scholarship on this important topic.

Next Steps

The three elements highlighted in the previous section are starting points for further answers to the central question of what happened to the women. This book has examined women choosing to work for peace as a conscious choice and form of political activism, sometimes driven by feminist goals and sometimes by more traditional values specifically as wife and mother. The primarily patriarchal structure of political decision-making excluded women from the initial decisions to engage in some form of political violence. Hence, women are put into a position of having to respond to that situation, not necessarily as victims, but as political actors. Working for peace is one of those options, as we and others have documented in determining the reasons for activism.

However, another response that some women choose is to become active participants in the conflict as combatants, perpetrating violence. Just as some women work for peace as a way to gain some control and political agency in a situation of conflict or war, others clearly opt to engage as belligerents. The question then becomes why some women choose one option while some other women choose the other. There are ample examples of women acting either in support of the conflict or resorting to acts of violence at various points along the continuum of violence. In some cases, in fact, it is the assumptions of gender norms or stereotyping that have allowed women to act in support of the conflict. As Miranda Alison states, "In many cases, women involved in nationalist struggles, while themselves undertaking non-traditional gender roles, have utilized conservative gender constructions and stereotypes to pursue their objectives against the state or their perceived enemy. In Afghanistan, Algeria and Palestine, for example, women have used local cultural expectations about what clothing is appropriate for them to secretly transport small arms and explosives."[6] In Northern Ireland women have used baby carriages to transport weapons, knowing that they would be less likely to be stopped and searched.[7] These gendered constructions put women into a unique position to act in support of the cause and to engage in actions that support the ongoing political violence generally beyond suspicion.

But there are also myriad examples of women who go beyond supporting the conflict in some way to engaging actively in acts of violence as combatants. As Bouta, Frerks, and Bannon note, women have actively participated in conflicts around the world, including female combatants in Algeria, El Salvador, Eritrea, Ethiopia, Mozambique, Namibia, Nepal, Nicaragua, South Africa, Sri Lanka, and Zimbabwe. Their numbers are not insignificant. They note that 25 percent of the combatants of El Salvador's Farabundo Marti National Liberation Front (FMLN) were women. In the case of Nicaragua, approximately "30 percent of soldiers and leaders of the Sandanista National Liberation Front" were female. In the case of women combatants in the FMLN, one of the interesting points that can be made is that many of the high-ranking women were also later involved in the peace negotiations although, as one noted, her involvement was not "as a woman, but as a representative of a powerful armed group."[8]

In cases such as El Salvador and Sudan, women filled leadership positions, both within the military or para-military structures as well as within the government. Bouta, Frerks, and Bannon also point out that "such gender changes at the micro level are often not accompanied by corresponding changes in political or organizational influence, and they do not fundamentally alter patriarchal ideologies."[9] Hence, while some women gained leadership positions *during* conflict, they were excluded from the decisions to engage in violence and were blocked from continuing in positions of political power and influence after the conflict ended. The exclusion of former women combatants in the post-conflict period is thus mirrored in the exclusion of women peace activists in peace negotiations.

In general, the image of women as combatants runs counter to established social and perceptual norms of women as peaceful and peace makers. But as feminist scholars have repeatedly shown, understandings of masculinity and femininity are socially and culturally constructed.[10] Using the Sri Lankan rebel group, the LTTE, as an example, Kim Jordan and Myriam Denov assert that "the LTTE's ideological commitment to women's liberation is translated into practice made visible through women's access to groundbreaking roles and responsibilities. In this way, the experiences of female soldiers underlie a disruption in conventional gender constructions."[11] They offer some caveats about what this means for women's roles and empowerment. For example, they say that "while public approval and rhetoric re-garding LTTE women suggests an acceptance of women 'as equals,' the glorifica-tion of the women fighters can be seen to reinforce the perception of females as *the symbolic nurturers of society*" (emphasis added). And they continue, "While females may benefit from more egalitarian relations within the LTTE than within tradi-tional Tamil society, women's empowerment is made possible through the adoption of masculine behaviors as opposed to consciously attempting to 'feminize' the mili-tary subculture. This reinforces the assertion that female actors are permitted in armed conflict as long as their exclusion does not disrupt the masculine image of warfare."[12]

The conclusion here is that engaging women as combatants has allowed some women to gain prominence and visibility in societies in which women traditionally held secondary roles. They did gain a certain amount of power and agency in being able to make decisions that allowed them to support a cause they believed in, and to do so in a way that was outside the traditional domain for women by taking an overtly public and aggressive stance. That said, they often took on these roles within a structure that was male dominated and that glorified violence as the appropriate means to an end. In that sense, women were asked to fit into an existing structure, which many have done quite well, rather than trying to change it.

Does this challenge the notion of women as nurturers and lovers of peace, of individuals who shy away from conflict? It seems to. But it also suggests that women are as capable of making a choice to engage in conflict, armed combat, and even suicide missions as men are for causes in which they believe. Women often pursue lives as combatants where they are blocked from participating in the formal politi-cal process, either overtly or covertly. Women as combatants, as is true of women's access in other areas of political decision-making, ultimately is dependent upon the decisions made by a patriarchal system even to allow them to participate. Whether women ultimately choose to do so then becomes their decision to make. Conse-quently, future research might consider exploring the question of why women choose violence as their form of political action as opposed to working for peace, and is it any different when women take such action than when men do?

Notes

[1] Cynthia Cockburn, "The Gendered Dynamics of Armed Conflict," in *Victims, Perpe-trators, or Actors? Gender, Armed Conflict, and Political Violence*, ed. Caroline O. N. Moser and Fiona C. Clark, 30–51 (London: Zed Books, 2001).

[2] Elissa Helms, "Women as Agents of Ethnic Reconciliation? Women's NGOs and In-ternational Intervention in Postwar Bosnia-Herzegovina," *Women's Studies International Forum* 26, no. 1 (2003): 20.

[3] Tsjeard Bouta, Georg Frerks, and Ian Bannon, *Gender, Conflict and Development* (Washington DC: The World Bank, 2004), 50–51.

[4] "Report of the Northern Ireland Women's Coalition Meeting held on Saturday 11th February 2006 in the Aisling Center, Enniskillen." Unpublished report, accessed at the Linen Hall Library, Belfast, Northern Ireland, NIWC archives, June 2008.

[5] Interview with Jane Morrice, November 21, 2007, Belfast, Northern Ireland.

[6] Miranda Alison, "Women as Agents of Political Violence: Gendering Security," *Security Dialogue* 35, no. 4 (December 2004): 456.

[7] Ibid., 457.

[8] Bouta, Frerks, and Bannon, *Gender, Conflict, and Development*, 11, 54.

[9] Ibid., 55.

[10] J. Ann Tickner, *Gendering World Politics* (New York: Columbia University Press, 2001), 15.

[11] Kim Jordan and Myriam Denov, "Birds of Freedom? Perspectives on Female Emancipation and Sri Lanka's Liberation Tigers of Tamil Eelam," *Journal of International Women's Studies* 9, no. 1 (November 2007): 57.

[12] Ibid., 57–58.

About the Authors

Joyce P. Kaufman is professor of political science and director of the Whittier Scholars Program at Whittier College. She is the author of *A Concise History of U.S. Foreign Policy* (Rowman and Littlefield Publishers, 2006) and *NATO and the Former Yugoslavia: Crisis, Conflict and the Atlantic Alliance* (Rowman and Littlefield Publishers, 2002), as well as numerous articles and papers on US foreign and security policy. With Kristen Williams, she is co-author of *Women, the State, and War: A Comparative Perspective on Citizenship and Nationalism* (Lexington Books, 2007). She received her BA and MA degrees from New York University and her PhD from the University of Maryland.

Kristen P. Williams is associate professor in the Department of Political Science and director of the Women's and Gender Studies Program at Clark University. She is the author of *Despite Nationalist Conflicts: Theory and Practice of Maintaining World Peace* (Praeger, 2001), *Identity and Institutions: Conflict Reduction in Divided Societies* (with Neal G. Jesse) (SUNY, 2005), and *Ethnic Conflict* (with Neal G. Jesse), as well as journal articles on nationalism and ethnic conflict, and gender and war. With Joyce Kaufman, she is co-author of *Women, the State, and War: A Comparative Perspective on Citizenship and Nationalism* (Lexington, 2007). She received her PhD from UCLA.

Selected Bibliography

Abdela, Lesley. "Kosovo: Missed Opportunities, Lessons for the Future." In Afshar and Eade, *Development, Women, and War*, 87–99.

"About the ICTY." http://www.icty.org/sid/3 (accessed June 7, 2009).

Afshar, Haleh. "Introduction (Part 1): What Do Women Contribute?" In Afshar and Eade, *Development, Women, and War*, 2.

————. "Women and Wars: Some Trajectories towards a Feminist Peace." In Afshar and Eade, *Development, Women, and War*, 43–59.

————. "Women and wars: some trajectories towards a feminist peace." *Development in Practice* 13, nos. 2/3 (May 2003): 178–88.

Afshar, Haleh, and Deborah Eade. *Development, Women, and War: Feminist Perspectives.* Oxford, England: Oxfam Publishing, 2004.

Alberdi, Ines. "UNIFEM Welcomes Security Council Resolutions 1888 and 1889," UNIFEM (October 5, 2009). Available on the www.unifem.org website.

Alison, Miranda. "Cogs in the Wheel? Women in the Liberation Tigers of Tamil Eelam," *Civil Wars* 6, no. 4 (Winter 2003): 37–54.

————. "Wartime Sexual Violence: Women's Human Rights and Questions of Masculinity." *Review of International Studies* 33, no. 1 (2007): 75–90.

————. "Women as Agents of Political Violence: Gendering Security." *Security Dialogue* 35, no. 4 (December 2004): 448–62.

Anderlini, Sanam Naraghi. *Women Building Peace: What They Do, Why It Matters.* Boulder, CO: Lynne Rienner, 2007.

————. *Women, Peace, and Security: A Policy Audit.* London: International Alert, June 2001.

————. "Women at the Peace Table: Making a Difference." New York: United Nations Development Fund for Women, 2000.

Aretxaga, Begona. *Shattering Silence: Women, Nationalism, and Political Subjectivity in Northern Ireland.* Princeton, NJ: Princeton University Press, 1997.

Baaz, Maria Eriksson, and Maria Stern. "Why Do Soldiers Rape? Masculinity, Violence, and Sexuality in the Armed Forces in the Congo (DRC)." *International Studies Quarterly* 53 (2009): 495–518.

Beckwith, Karen. "Beyond Compare? Women's Movements in Comparative Perspective." *European Journal of Political Research* 37 (2000): 431–68.

————. "The Comparative Politics of Women's Movements," *Perspectives on Politics* 3, no. 3 (September 2005): 583–96.

Beckwith, Karen, and Kimberley Cowell-Meyers. "Sheer Numbers: Critical Representation Thresholds and Women's Political Representation." *Perspectives on Politics* 5, no. 3 (September 2007): 553–65.

Black Sash. http://www.blacksash.org.za.

Blood, May (Baroness). *Watch My Lips, I'm Speaking.* Dublin: Gill and MacMillan, 2007.

Bose, Sumantra. *Contested Lands: Israel-Palestine, Kashmir, Bosnia, Cyprus, and Sri Lanka.* Cambridge, MA: Harvard University Press, 2007.

Bouta, Tsjeard, Georg Frerks, and Ian Bannon. *Gender, Conflict, and Development.* Washington DC: The World Bank, 2004.

Callaway, Helen. "Survival and Support: Women's Forms of Political Action." In Ridd and Callaway, *Caught Up in Conflict,* 214–30.

Campbell, Patricia J. "Gender and Post-Conflict Civil Society." *International Feminist Journal of Politics* 7, no. 3 (September 2005): 377–99.

Caprioli, Mary, and Kimberly Lynn Douglass. "Nation Building and Women: The Effect of Intervention on Women's Agency." *Foreign Policy Analysis* 4 (2008): 45–65.

Chenoy, Anuradha M. "Militarization, Conflict, and Women in South Asia." In Lorentzen and Turpin, *The Women and War Reader,* 101–10.

Chinkin, Christine, and Hilary Charlesworth. "Building Women into Peace: The International Legal Framework." *Third World Quarterly* 27, no.5 (2006): 937–57.

Cock, Jacklyn. "Closing the Circle: Towards a Gendered Understanding of War and Peace" (July 2001). Available on the wb.uct.ac.za website.

———. *Women and War in South Africa.* Cleveland, OH: Pilgrim Press, 1993.

Cockburn, Cynthia. "The Continuum of Violence: A Gender Perspective on War and Peace." In Giles and Hyndman, *Sites of Violence,* 24–44.

———. *From Where We Stand: War, Women's Activism and Feminist Analysis.* London: Zed Books, 2007.

———. "The Gendered Dynamics of Armed Conflict." In Moser and Clark, *Victims, Perpetrators, or Actors?* 13–29.

———. *The Line: Women, Partition and the Gender Order in Cyprus.* London: Zed Books, 2004.

———. *The Space between Us: Negotiating Gender and National Identities in Conflict.* London: Zed Books, 1998.

Cohen, J. "Women in Peace and War." In *Psychological Factors of Peace and War,* ed. Tom Hatherly Pear, 92–110. Freeport, NY: Books for Libraries Press, 1971.

Coomaraswamy, Radhika. "A Question of Honour: Women, Ethnicity, and Armed Conflict." In *Feminists under Fire: Exchanges across War Zones,* ed. Wenona Giles, Malathi de Alwis, Edith Klein, and Neluka Silva, with Maja Korac, Djurdja Knezevic, and Zarana Papic, 91–101. Toronto: Between the Lines, 2003.

Copelon, Rhonda. "Surfacing Gender: Reconceptualizing Crimes against Women in Time of War." In Lorentzen and Turpin, *The Women and War Reader,* 63–79.

Cordero, Isabel Coral. "Social Organizations: From Victims to Actors in Peace Building." In Moser and Clark, *Victims, Perpetrators, or Actors?* 151–63.

Corrin, Chris. "Post-Conflict Reconstruction and Gender Analysis in Kosova." *International Feminist Journal of Politics* 3, no. 1 (2000): 78–98.

Crawley, Heaven. "Engendering the State in Refugee Women's Claims for Asylum." In Jacobs, Jacobson, and Marchbank, *States of Conflict*, 87–104.

Devlin, Bernadette. *The Price of My Soul.* New York: Vintage Books, 1969.

Eduards, Maud L. "Women's Agency and Collective Action." *Women's Studies International Forum* 17, nos. 2/3 (1994): 181–86.

El-Bushra, Judy. "Transforming Conflict: Some Thoughts on a Gendered Understanding of Conflict Processes." In Jacobs, Jacobson, and Marchbank, *States of Conflict*, 66–86.

Emmett, Ayala. *Our Sisters' Promised Land: Women, Politics, and Israeli-Palestinian Coexistence.* Ann Arbor: University of Michigan Press, 2003.

Enloe, Cynthia. "All the Men Are in the Militias, All the Women Are Victims: The Politics of Masculinity and Femininity in Nationalist Wars." In Lorentzen and Turpin, *The Women and War Reader*, 50–62.

———. *Bananas, Beaches, and Bases: Making Feminist Sense of International Relations.* Berkeley and Los Angeles: University of California Press, 1989.

———. *Maneuvers: The International Politics of Militarizing Women's Lives.* Berkeley and Los Angeles: University of California Press, 2000.

Fattah, Hassan M. "Kuwait Grants Political Rights to Its Women." *The New York Times*, May 17, 2005.

Fearon, Kate. *Women's Work: The Story of the Northern Ireland Women's Coalition.* Belfast: Blackstaff Press, 1999.

Freedman, Jane. "Women Seeking Asylum: The Politics of Gender in the Asylum Determination Process in France." *International Feminist Journal of Politics* 10, no. 2 (June 2008): 154–72.

Galtung, Johann. "Violence, Peace, and Peace Research." *Journal of Peace Research* 6, no. 3 (1969): 167–91.

Giles, Wenona, and Jennifer Hyndman, eds. *Sites of Violence: Gender and Conflict Zones.* Berkeley and Los Angeles: University of California Press, 2004.

Gobodo-Madikizela, Pumla. "Women's Contributions to South Africa's Truth and Reconciliation Commission." Women Waging Peace Policy Commission, February 2005.

Goldstein, Joshua S. *War and Gender: How Gender Shapes the War System and Vice Versa.* Cambridge: Cambridge University Press, 2001.

Hassim, Shireen. *Women's Organizations and Democracy in South Africa: Contesting Authority.* Madison: The University of Wisconsin Press, 2006.

Helms, Elissa. "Gender Essentialisms and Women's Activism in Post-War Bosnia-Herzegovina." In *Feminists under Fire: Exchanges across War Zones*, ed. Wenona Giles, Malathi de Alwis, Edith Klein, and Neluka Silva with Maja Korac, Djurdja Knezevic, and Zarana Papic, 181–93. Toronto: Between the Lines, 2003.

———. "Women as Agents of Ethnic Reconciliation? Women's NGOs and International Intervention in Postwar Bosnia-Herzegovina." *Women's Studies International Forum* 26, no. 1 (2003): 15–33.

Holsti, K. J. *International Relations: A Framework for Analysis*, 7th ed. Englewood Cliffs, NJ: Prentice Hall, 1995.

Human Rights Watch. "UN: Take Action against Rape in War" (May 25, 2008). Available on the www.hrw.org website.

Human Rights Watch. "Uncertain Refuge: International Failures to Protect Refugees," *Human Rights Watch Short Report* 9, no. 1 (April 1997): 9.

Hunt, Swanee. "Moving beyond Silence: Women Waging Peace." In *Listening to the Silences: Women and War,* ed. Helen Durham and Tracy Gurd, 251–71. The Netherlands: Koninklijke Brill BV, 2005.

Hunt, Swanee, and Cristina Posa. "Women Waging Peace." *Foreign Policy* 124 (May-June 2001): 38–47.

Hyndman, Jennifer. "Refugee Camps as Conflict Zones: The Politics of Gender." In Giles and Hyndman, *Sites of Violence*, 193–212.

"International Alliance of Women, Records of the Southeast Regional Seminar." Colombo, Sri Lanka, November 6–11, 1975 (accessed at the Women's Library, London, June 2008).

"International Criminal Tribunal for Rwanda." http://www.ictr.org/default.htm (accessed June 7, 2009).

Jacobs, Susie, Ruth Jacobson, and Jennifer Marchbank, eds. *States of Conflict: Gender, Violence, and Resistance*. London: Zed Books, 2000.

Jacobson, Ruth, Susie Jacobs, and Jennifer Marchbank. "Introduction: States of Conflict." In Jacobs, Jacobson, and Marchbank, *States of Conflict*, 1–23.

Jacoby, Tami Amanda. *Women in Zones of Conflict: Power and Resistance in Israel*. Quebec: McGill-Queen's University Press, 2005.

Jamal, Amina. "Feminist 'Selves' and Feminism's 'Others': Feminist Representations of Jamaat-e-Islami Women in Pakistan." *Feminist Review* 81 (2005): 52–73.

Jaquette, Jane S. "Women and Democracy: Regional Differences and Contrasting Views." *Journal of Democracy* 12, no. 3 (July 2001): 111–25.

Jordan, Kim, and Myriam Denov. "Birds of Freedom? Perspectives on Female Emancipation and Sri Lanka's Liberation Tigers of Tamil Eelam." *Journal of International Women's Studies* 9, no.1 (November 2007): 42–62.

Karam, Azza. "Women in War and Peace-building." *International Feminist Journal of Politics* 3, no. 1 (April 2001): 2–25.

Kaufman, Joyce P., and Kristen P. Williams. "Who Belongs? Women, Marriage, and Citizenship," *International Feminist Journal of Politics* 6, no. 3 (September 2004): 416–35.

———. *Women, the State, and War: A Comparative Perspective on Citizenship and Nationalism*. Lanham, MD: Lexington Books, 2007.

Kelly, Liz. "Wars against Women: Sexual Violence, Sexual Politics, and the Militarized State." In Jacobs, Jacobson, and Marchbank, *States of Conflict*, 45–65.

Korac, Maja. "Gender, Conflict, and Peace-Building: Lessons from the Conflict in the Former Yugoslavia." *Women's Studies International Forum* 29 (2006): 511–20.

Kumar, Krishna, ed. *Women and Civil War: Impact, Organizations, and Action*. Boulder, CO: Lynne Rienner, 2001.

Kumar, Krishna, Hannah Baldwin, and Judy Benjamin. "Profile: Cambodia." In Kumar, *Women and Civil War*, 39–47.

Kvinna till Kvinna. *Engendering the Peace Process: A Gender Approach to Dayton—and Beyond*. Stockholm: The Kvinna till Kvinna Foundation, 2000.

Leiby, Michele L. "Wartime Sexual Violence in Guatemala and Peru." *International Studies Quarterly* 53 (2009): 445–68.

Liebergman, Amy. "UN Appoints Wallstrom Special Representative for Sexual Violence." *Europa Newswire* (February 9, 2010). Available on the www.europanewsblog.com website.

Lister, Ruth. "Feminist Citizenship Theory: An Alternative Perspective on Understanding Women's Social and Political Lives," paper presented at Women and Social Capital, London South Bank University, April 2005.

Lorentzen, Lois Ann, and Jennifer Turpin, eds. *The Women and War Reader*. New York: New York University Press, 1998.

McAliskey, Bernadette Devlin. "From Rural to Urban: A Rural View," talk given at the Peace by Piece: Three Day International Women's Conference. Belfast, Northern Ireland, June 25, 2008.

McKeown, Laurence, and Simona Sharoni. "Formations and Transformations of Masculinity in the North of Ireland and in Israel-Palestine." Unpublished paper. 2002.

McWilliams, Monica. "Struggling for Peace and Justice: Reflections on Women's Activism in Northern Ireland." *Journal of Women's History* 6/7, nos. 4/1 (Winter/Spring 1995): 13–39.

Meintjes, Sheila, Anu Pillay, and Meredith Tershen. "There Is No Aftermath for Women." In *The Aftermath: Women in Post-Conflict Transformation*, ed. Sheila Meintjes, Anu Pillay, and Meredith Tershen, 3–18. London: Zed Books, 2001.

Mertus, Julie A. *War's Offensive on Women: The Humanitarian Challenge in Bosnia, Kosovo, and Afghanistan*. Bloomfield, CT: Kumarian Press, 2000.

Mills, Paula. "Working to Promote 1325 in Israel: Opportunities and Challenges Facing Activist Women and Isha L'Isha." Working Paper, The Boston Consortium on Gender, Security, and Human Rights, November 29, 2006.

Morgenthau, Hans J. *Politics among Nations: The Struggle for Power and Peace*. Revised by Kenneth W. Thompson. Boston: McGraw Hill, 1993.

Moser, Caroline O. N., and Fiona C. Clark, eds. *Victims, Perpetrators, or Actors? Gender, Armed Conflict, and Political Violence*. London: Zed Books, 2001.

NIWC. Education Policy Team. "Education for the Twenty-first Century: The Report of the Post-Primary Review Body," June 2002. Unpublished report, accessed at the Linen Hall Library, Belfast, NIWC archives, June 2008.

Nye, Joseph. *The Paradox of American Power: Why the World's Only Superpower Can't Go It Alone*. New York: Oxford University Press, 2002.

Office of the United Nations High Commission for Human Rights, "The Convention relating to the Status of Refugees" (July 28, 1951). http://www.2.ohchr.org/english/law/refugees.htm (accessed March 9, 2010).

———. "Refugee Women." http://www.unhcr.org/pages/49c3646c1d9.html.

O'Meara, Louise. "Additional Measures Required to Address the Issue of the Under-represented Women in Political Life," unpublished report prepared by the Northern Ireland Voluntary Trust, December 1997, accessed at the Linen Hall Library, Belfast, June 2008.

Pankhurst, Donna. "The 'Sex War' and Other Wars: Towards a Feminist Approach to Peace Building." *Development in Practice* 13, nos. 2/3 (May 2003): 154–77.

———. "Women, Gender, and Peacebuilding." Working Paper 5. Center for Conflict Resolution. Bradford, UK: University of Bradford, August 2000.

Peterson, V. Spike. "Gendered Nationalism: Reproducing 'Us' versus 'Them.'" In Lorentzen and Turpin, *The Women and War Reader*, 41–49.

———, ed. *Gendered States: Feminist (Re)Visions of International Relations Theory*. Boulder, CO: Lynne Rienner, 1992.

———. "The Politics of Identity in International Relations." *The Fletcher Forum of World Affairs* 17, no. 2 (1993): 1–12.

———. "Sexing Political Identities/Nationalism as Heterosexism." *International Feminist Journal of Politics* 1, no. 1 (1999): 34–65.

Peterson, V. Spike, and Anne Sisson Runyan. *Global Gender Issues*. Boulder, CO: Westview Press, 1993, 1999.

Porter, Elisabeth. "The Challenge of Dialogue across Difference." In *Gender, Democracy, and Inclusion in Northern Ireland*, ed. Carmel Roulston and Celia Davis, 141–63. New York, Palgrave, 2001.

———. "Creating Dialogical Spaces in Northern Ireland." *International Feminist Journal of Politics* 2, no. 2 (Summer 2000): 163–84.

———. "Identity, Location, Plurality: Women, Nationalism, and Northern Ireland." In *Women, Ethnicity, and Nationalism: The Politics of Transition*, ed. Rick Wilford and Robert L. Miller, 36–61. New York: Routledge, 1998.

———. "Women, Political Decision-Making, and Peace-Building." *Global Change, Peace and Security* 15, no. 3 (October 2003): 245–62.

Records of the International Alliance of Women, 1904–1991, archived August 2005 (accessed at the Women's Library, London, June 2008).

Regan, Patrick M., and Aida Paskeviciute. "Women's Access to Politics and Peaceful States." *Journal of Peace Research* 40, no. 3 (2003): 287–302.

"Report of the Northern Ireland Women's Coalition Meeting Held on Saturday 11th February 2006 in the Aisling Centre, Enniskillen." Unpublished, accessed at the Linen Hall Library, archives of the NIWC, June 2008.

Richter-Devore, Sophie. "Gender, Culture, and Conflict Resolution in Palestine." *Journal of Middle East Women's Studies* 4, no. 2 (Spring 2008): 30–59.

Ridd, Rosemary. "Powers of the Powerless." In Ridd and Callaway, *Caught Up in Conflict*, 1–24.

Ridd, Rosemary, and Helen Callaway, eds. *Caught Up in Conflict: Women's Responses to Political Strife*. London: Macmillan, 1986.

Roulston, Carmel. "Women on the Margin: The Women's Movement in Northern Ireland, 1973–1995." In *Feminist Nationalism*, ed. Lois West, 41–58. New York: Routledge, 1997.

Sapiro, Virginia. "Research Frontier Essay: When Are Interests Interesting? The Problem of Political Representation of Women." *American Political Science Review* 75, no. 3 (September 1981): 701–16.

Shearer, Norma. "A Helping Hand," talk given at Peace by Piece, International Women's Conference, June 24, 2008, Belfast, Northern Ireland.

Sideris, Tina. "Problems of Identity, Solidarity and Reconciliation." In *The Aftermath: Women in Post-Conflict Transformation*, ed. Sheila Meintjes, Anu Pillay, and Meredith Tershen, 46–62. London: Zed Books, 2001.

Singer, J. David. "The Level-of-Analysis Problem in International Relations." *World Politics* 14, no. 1 (October 1961): 77–92.

Sjoberg, Laura, and Caron E. Gentry. *Mothers, Monsters, and Whores: Women's Violence in Global Politics*. London: Zed Books, 2007.

Skjelsbaek, Inger. "Gendered Battlefields: A Gender Analysis of Peace and Conflict." PRIO report. Oslo, Norway: International Peace Research Institute, October 1997.

————. "Is Femininity Inherently Peaceful? The Construction of Femininity in War." In *Gender, Peace, and Conflict*, ed. Inger Skjelsbaek and Dan Smith, 47–67. London: Sage, 2001.

Slackman, Michael. "A Quiet Revolution in Algeria: Gains by Women." *The New York Times,* May 26, 2007: A1, A6.

Smith, Dan. "The Problem of Essentialism." In *Gender, Peace and Conflict*, ed. Inger Skjelsbaek and Dan Smith, 32–46. London: Sage, 2001.

Tershen, Meredith. "Engendernig Relations of State to Society in the Aftermath." In *The Aftermath: Women in Post-Conflict Transformation*, ed. Sheila Meintjes, Anu Pillay, and Meredith Tershen, 78–96. London: Zed Books, 2001.

Thomas, Dorothy Q., and Regan E. Ralph. "Rape in War: The Case of Bosnia." In *Gender Politics in the Western Balkans: Women and Society in Yugoslavia and the Yugoslav Successor States*, ed. Sabrina P. Ramet, 203–18. University Park: The Pennsylvania State University Press, 1999.

Thompson, Martha, and Deborah Eade. "Women and War: Protection through Empowerment in El Salvador." In Afshar and Eade, *Development, Women, and War*, 220–37.

Tickner, J. Ann. "Feminism Meets International Relations: Some Methodological Issues." In *Feminist Methodologies for International Relations*, ed. Brooke A. Ackerly, Maria Stern, and Jacqui True, 19–41. Cambridge: Cambridge University Press, 2006.

————. *Gender in International Relations: Feminists Perspectives on Achieving Global Security.* New York: Columbia University Press, 1992.

————. *Gendering World Politics: Issues and Approaches in the Post–Cold War Era.* New York: Columbia University Press, 2001.

————. "You Just Don't Understand: Troubled Engagements between Feminists and IR Theorists." *International Studies Quarterly* 41 (1997): 611–32.

Tilly, Charles. *Coercion, Capital, and European States; AD 990–1992.* Cambridge, MA: Blackwell Publishers, 1992.

Turpin, Jennifer. "Many Faces: Women Confronting War." In Lorentzen and Turpin, *The Women and War Reader*, 3–18.

United Nations. "Secretary-General Appoints Margot Wallström of Sweden as Special Representative on Sexual Violence in Conflict." United Nations, Department of Public Information (February 2, 2010).

United Nations Division for the Advancement of Women and International Peace Research Institute (Oslo). Expert Group Meeting. "Political Decision-Making and Conflict Resolution: The Impact of Gender Difference." Santo Domingo, Dominican Republic, October 1996.

United Nations High Commissioner for Refugees (written by Erin K. Baines). *Respect Our Rights: Partnership for Equality: Report on the Dialogue with Refugee Women, June 20–22, 2001* (December 2001).

United Nations Office for the Coordination of Humanitarian Affairs. "Human Security," United Nations (2007).

United Nations Security Council, Resolution 1325 (October 31, 2000). http:\\www.peacewomen.org/un/sc/1325.html.

———. "Security Council Demands Immediate and Complete Halt to Acts of Sexual Violence against Civilians in Conflict Zones, Unanimously Adopting Resolution 1820 (2008)," SC/9364, United Nations Department of Public Information (June 19, 2008). Available on the www.un.org website.

Waltz, Kenneth N. *Man, the State, and War: A Theoretical Analysis.* New York: Columbia University Press, 1959.

Ward, Margaret. "Gender, Citizenship, and the Future of the Northern Ireland Peace Process." *Irish Feminist Studies* 41, nos. 1/2 (Spring/Summer 2006): 262–83.

Ward, Rachel. *Women, Unionism, and Loyalism in Northern Ireland: From "Tea-Makers" to Political Actors.* Dublin: Irish Academic Press, 2006.

Werbner, Pnina, and Nira Yuval-Davis. "Introduction: Women and the New Discourse of Citizenship." In *Women, Citizenship, and Difference,* ed. Nira Yuval-Davis and Pnina Werber, 1–38. London: Zed Books, 1999.

Westervelt, Eric. "Middle East: Female Activists a Force in Male-Dominated Gaza." National Public Radio, *Morning Edition,* January 6, 2007. Available on the www.npr.org website.

Women in Black. http://www.womeninblack.net/mission.html (accessed December 20, 2007).

Women's Refugee Commission. *Peril or Protection: The Link between Livelihoods and Gender-based Violence in Displacement Settings.* New York: Women's Refugee Commission, November 2009.

Workshop on Peace through Human Rights and Understanding, Navan, Ireland, October 12–17, 1986. Workshop summary, accessed at the Women's Library, London, June 2008.

York, Jennifer. "The Truth about Women and Peace." In Lorentzen and Turpin, *The Women and War Reader,* 19–25.

Youngs, Gillian. "Feminist International Relations: A Contradiction in Terms? Or: Why Women and Gender Are Essential to Understanding the World 'We' Live In." *International Affairs* 80, no. 1 (2004): 75–87.

Youngs, Gillian. *International Relations in a Global Age: A Conceptual Challenge.* Cambridge: Polity, 1999.

Yuval-Davis, Nira. "Gender, the Nationalist Imagination, War, and Peace." In Giles and Hyndman, *Sites of Violence*, 170–89.

———. "Women, Citizenship, and Difference." *Feminist Review* 57 (1997): 4–27.

Zuckerman, Elaine, and Marcia Greenberg. "The Gender Dimensions of Post-Conflict Reconstruction: An Analytical Framework for Policymakers." *Gender and Development* 12, no. 3 (November 2004): 70–82.

Index

Also from Kumarian Press...

Conflict & Peacebuilding:

For the Love of God: NGOs and Religious Identity in a Violent World
Shawn Flanigan

Building Peace: Practical Reflections from the Field
Edited by Craig Zelizer and Robert Rubinstein

All Her Paths Are Peace: Women Pioneers in Peacemaking
Michael Henderson

Policy, Politics & Gender: Women Gaining Ground
Kathleen Staudt

New and Forthcoming:

Dispossessed People: Establishing Legitimacy and Rights for Global Migrants
Christine Ho and James Loucky

Schools in the Forest: How Grassroots Education Brought Political
Empowerment to the Brazilian Amazon
Denis Heyck

Artisans and Fair Trade: Crafting Development
Mary Littrell and Marsha Dickson

Strategic Moral Diplomacy: Understanding the Enemy's Moral Universe
Lyn Boyd-Judson

Visit Kumarian Press at **www.kpbooks.com** or
call **toll-free 800.232.0223** for a complete catalog.

Kumarian Press, located in Sterling, Virginia, is a forward-looking, scholarly press that promotes active international engagement and an awareness of global connectedness.